spice/a cook's companion

For my lovely mum.

Cook's notes
Eggs are medium, and free-range, unless otherwise stated
Parsley is always flat-leaf
Sea salt is used throughout
Extra virgin olive oil is used throughout

Publishing Director Sarah Lavelle
Commissioning Editor Harriet Webster
Head of Design Claire Rochford
Design Matt Cox at Newman+Eastwood Ltd.
Cover Design and Illustration Matt Cox
Photographer Mark Diacono
Food Stylists Matt Williamson and Mark Diacono
Head of Production Stephen Lang
Production Controller Sabeena Atchia

Published in 2022 by Quadrille, an imprint of Hardie Grant Publishing

Quadrille
52–54 Southwark Street
London SE1 1UN
quadrille.com

Cataloguing in Publication Data: a catalogue record for this book is available from the British Library.

Text © Mark Diacono 2022
Photography © Mark Diacono 2022
Design © Quadrille 2022

Recipe on pages 80–82 © MiMi Aye, 2022. MiMi Aye has asserted
    her right to be identified as the author of the recipe.
Recipe on pages 90–92 © Yemisi Aribisala, 2021
Recipe on pages 118–120 © Irina Georgescu, 2021
Recipe on pages 158–160 © Yuki Gomi, 2022
Recipe on pages 166–167 © Li Ling Wang, 2022
Recipe on pages 170–171 © Lara Lee, 2022
Recipe on pages 176–177 © Maunika Gowardhan, 2022
Recipe on pages 180–181 © José Pizarro, 2022
Recipe on pages 184–185 © Annie Gray, 2022
Recipes on pages 188–189 and 196–197 © Sumayya Usmani, 2022
Recipe on pages 200–201 © Zuza Zak, 2022
Recipe on pages 214–215 © Alissa Timoshkina, 2022
Recipe on pages 218–220 © Nicola Miller, 2022
Recipe on pages 224–225 © Nargisse Benkabbou, 2022
Recipe on pages 232–233 © Sarit Packer, Honey & Co., 2022

ISBN 978 1 78713 643 4

Printed in China

MIX
Paper from
responsible sources
FSC™ C020056
FSC
www.fsc.org

spice/a cook's companion

MARK DIACONO

Hardie Grant

QUADRILLE

CONTENTS

INTRODUCTION

Until the first supermarket came to town, there were only two spices in the house: a small pot of white pepper and a tall jar of small, dark red chillies Dad kept in an old Nescafé jar. Every Saturday, when we got back from doing The Big Shop, the scent of chillies and cheap mince hitting hot lard would reach my bedroom. Even from there, I could tell when he added the first of many shakes from the small pot of white pepper.

The supermarket widened our spice world in only one respect: mixed spice entered the house. A jar sat – next to another of mixed herbs – on the shelf in the cold cobwebby larder. My mum would dust the apple filling of a pie heavily with it before bringing down the lid on the pastry coffin. She would always pop it in the oven while we were eating Sunday lunch and every time I'd be sure I'd not be hungry by the time it came out, and every time the spicy scent of that pie filling the house had my stomach rumbling before the drying up from the roast was done.

Despite the decades, I can still recall how it felt like the pepper and the mixed spice put a shine on things and made them sit up: like when the optician tweaks the apparatus by your temple and the fourth row comes sharply into view. This is the brilliance of spices: they are – like music, painting and poetry – almost entirely unnecessary and yet utterly essential. As with herbs, spices transform the life-giving act of feeding into the life-enhancing pleasure of eating.

I have spent the years since the old man's eye-watering weekend curries exploring the ever-increasing wealth of spices easily available to us: I've grown around a third of the spices included in this book; the spice routes that once took months to bring flavours across the planet have been replaced by a couple of clicks and next-day delivery. What a joy to have these flavours at our fingertips. It wasn't always so. Humans have travelled, fought, colonized, bought and bribed in the name of spice. The history of civilization can be told in great part by our relationship with spices.

So widespread is our love for spice that attempting to write an exhaustive volume that shares recipes and blends from every food culture is doomed. Which is not to say I haven't covered plenty of ground. That said, this book has many aims and they are largely concerned with sharing an enthusiasm, building confidence and bringing pleasure; it is high on ideas, blends recipes (around 150, using spices that are familiar and some less so) and quite low on the historic movement of spices around the world, the wars fought and what might or might not have been rammed up Ramses II's nose before he was laid to rest.*

Many of us feel a degree of intimidation when it comes to using spices: we know they can embellish, enhance and catalyze but experience tells us they are easily mis-deployed, that a handful of ground cloves can deliver a lifetime of Christmases in a single mouthful of mince pie. This book will help.

There are forty-odd spices and a similar number of spice blends from around the world; some you will know, others not. What has made it past my ill-applied rules (see The Bouncer at the Door, page 10) of what is a spice and what is not is gathered together in The Spice Cabinet section. It will make friends of any spices that might not be regulars in your kitchen and offer some starting points about how you might use them all.

If you are not sure where to start, try the gin, the aquavit or the nutmeg brandy Alexander towards the back of the book: a good nip of any of those and you should feel ready to jump into any recipe.

*Black peppercorns, since you ask

THE BOUNCER AT THE DOOR

So much of the task of writing this book has been containing my enthusiasms for what seems like an unlimited array of flavours and aromas. I've had to make some hard choices about what to acknowledge as a spice and what to exclude.

As a basis, I've taken the spirit of my previous book *Herb* and applied it in reverse; this book deals largely with seeds and dried fruits, rather than leaves. It has led to some arguable calls: I include ground ginger and turmeric as spices, while discounting their fresh incarnations. Allow them in and garlic must come too, followed on a loose chain of logic by horseradish and other big-flavoured vegetables and fruit. And yet I have welcomed tamarind in. There have been testing questions: are sesame seeds a spice? Surely if juniper is in, why not barberries or myrtle berries? Rose petals? Rose water? Salt, even? Hmmm, maybe, I see your point, I guess you could … and yet no. I've left out the odd one on grounds of crapness of flavour: yes mastic, I'm looking at you. This is a personal selection, with all the bias, contradiction and inconsistency that implies. Imperfect as it may be, it is just about defensible.

AUTHENTICITY

In what can sometimes be a very binary world, I'm increasingly in favour of holding two or more seemingly part-contradictory thoughts in my mind and allowing them to coexist.

I very much believe that the kitchen is a place where cultures overlap, where ingredients not traditionally brought together can be thrown into an unfamiliar alliance that may prove holy or otherwise. If you want to sprinkle garam masala on your fried eggs, or add it to the salt for the rim of that third ill-advised tequila, no one should stop you. The spirit of play should be undiluted in the kitchen. I am far from new to the business of cooking and food writing, and I have much to say about spices and how to use them: I enthusiastically claim the right to respectfully play with ideas from cultures other than my own and to enjoy the spaces between.

That said, I cannot hope to fully represent the depth and breadth of food cultures around the world and I respect the importance of moving positively towards a better future when it comes to cultural appropriation. It struck me that this book might be enriched and those cultures respected if I was to beg, bribe, badger and cajole some of those whose food I love. I hope the food they call home offers you a springboard or two from which to leap. I am beyond grateful to those who have so generously shared their brilliance in these pages.

I have tried to cast a line to disparate geographical locations: I have largely succeeded. There are inevitably gaps, largely where attempts to find an authentic voice willing to contribute proved unsuccessful. I particularly regret bring unable to secure representation from the indigenous communities of America and Australia.

I am thrilled at what everyone has brought to the book. They have brought food cultures as diverse as Indonesia, Romania and Nigeria alive in these pages. I have enthusiastically played in the spaces between, and frequently placed more than a foot into territory beyond my home. It is done with love, open arms and is respectful of those in whose steps I tread. To some degree, the spirit of the old line about comedy being tragedy plus time applies to authenticity in food: cinnamon buns have a lead spice not grown within thousands of miles of Scandinavia, yet – thanks to time and repetition – it is one of the first recipes that springs to mind when I think of that region. My job isn't to only be true to the traditional: it's to go beyond, to offer different and new avenues to explore, and to respect and communicate the traditions and cultures on which we all do our thing, while encouraging you to do yours.

An example of where I think this works well: the first time I made niter kibbeh (page 68) – an Ethiopian spiced clarified butter – it inspired me to scribble a list of where I wanted to use it: a thick spoonful allowed to melt into very well done crumpets, stirred through rice in a kedgeree, on baked potatoes, to fry an egg in, to baste a sizzling steak with; and on it went. None are overly authentic to its Ethiopian heritage, and no less delicious for it. But that first taste also made me want to explore the food of that country even more, and that is one of the pleasures of this kind of fishing: you never know what you will pull out of the water on the end of your line, or indeed when it will drag you off the bank into the current that takes you somewhere unexpected.

THE SPICE CABINET

SOURCING AND USING

We cooks are often looking for the golden ticket to improve the flavour and pleasure in our food. In my experience, the greatest shift you can make is in allowing yourself a little more time – doing away with the sense of rush in the kitchen – so that your attention is more present. Secondly, valuing the importance of those small tweaks, the little differences, that may only add 1 per cent here, 2 per cent there, but together make the shift from pretty good to truly delicious.

First up, buy good ingredients. You don't always need the finest Tellicherry black pepper, but where pepper is more than a background hum you will tell the difference if you use it. Despite a shift in quality and breadth available in our shops and supermarkets, the finest spices are largely sourced online. I've made a list of suppliers I hope you will find useful (page 266). Each of these has supplied me with spice I've not only found uplifted my cooking, but the shift in quality has led to me actively thinking what I might make with this particular chilli or that black cardamom. Good spices can reverse the notion that they are the accompaniment, the flourish around the main character: they become the inspiration, the heart of the dish itself.

Buy whole spices where possible. Keep them in airtight containers out of direct sunlight. Grind any that are to be used as powder when you need them, as – to varying degrees – much of their essential character is lost in the days and weeks that follow. Buy some small jars for storing your own spice blends: having small quantities of a range of blends ready to go encourages you to use them on a whim.

Buy an electric grinder. As cute as a pestle and mortar is, and as useful as it can be for certain recipes, the novelty of picking up hard achiote or coriander seeds that once again have flicked from the mortar and almost blinded the dog quickly wears off. That said, the pleasure of using a suribachi and surikogi – the ridged bowl and pounding stick of Japan – to reduce spices to anything from gravel to dust brings its own reward.

There are many methods of using spices, all of which are featured in the recipe pages. The most common, opposite.

Marinades

A marinade is a paste, sauce or liquid that is applied (usually to meat or fish) for a period of time ahead of cooking, with the intention of imparting a deeper flavouring than if just mixed together. Depending on the marinade, it may also have the effect of tenderizing the meat or fish.

Rubs

These can act as either a dry form of marinade if left for a period of time, or as a surface flavouring ahead of being cooked.

Cooked

Many spices – cinnamon being one – release the full complexity of their flavour over a period of cooking. The allspice used in bigos (page 201), and the cinnamon or cassia used in many curries and stews are great examples of where cooking time brings spicy reward.

Tempering

Where spices – usually whole – are lightly cooked to release the flavours and aromas, separately to being used in a recipe. They may be fried in oil or ghee (sometimes with garlic and/or ginger) or dry-toasted in a pan. In both cases, the prepared spices may be added at the start of cooking, or to serve.

Added late/to serve

Many spices and spice blends give of their best or offer different qualities when not subjected to heat for long periods. Garam masala is a classic example: used early in the cooking process, it can bring a pleasing depth; added late, its subtleties are retained in the taste.

Infusions

As with herbs, there are occasions where you want to steal the flavour and aroma of a spice without eating it. The gin, aquavit and syrup recipes all show this to great effect.

ACHIOTE

Blends
Recado rojo

Affinities
Beef
Chicken
Chillies
Chocolate
Citrus
Eggs
Fish
Onions
Pork
Pulses
Rice
Squash
Stews
Sweetcorn
Tomatoes

The South American tree that gives us achiote – aka annatto – is quite the beauty, with clusters of bright red fruit held at the branch's fingertips, inside which are a few dozen seeds, long prized for the flavour and dye. Achiote seeds have a very gentle earthy pepperiness, with a faint sweet, minty scent; they are used perhaps more commonly to impart their colour – the definition of where red becomes orange – to sauces, smoked cheese and more. The Mayans of Central America used achiote's vividness as body paint for battle, so beware its dyeing qualities on anything white within 450 metres.

Using
Look for seed that is deeply rust coloured; bold and vivid, rather than too brown. The seeds have a long shelf life, but lose vibrance and flavour quickly when ground, so grind them – after soaking in water (unless you have a powerful electric grinder) as they are so hard – as you need them. Hot water or fat take the colour well: the seeds are warmed in the liquid and then discarded, and the liquid used to colour stews, rice and so on. Their flavour infuses best in warm oil. Achiote is occasionally available in ground form, which, though milder in flavour, releases its colour even more readily: recado rojo, a Mexican spice paste commonly used for meat and fish dishes including pollo pibil, uses ground achiote. It is a crucial ingredient to one of Mexico's many excellent chocolate drinks, tascalate (page 265).

Pictured opposite.

AJOWAN

Blends
Berbere
Chaat masala

Affinities
Beans
Bread
Chickpeas
Eggs
Fish
Onions
Pastry
Potatoes
Pulses
Root vegetables
Seafood

Spelled in a multitude of ways, ajowan is the seed of *Trachyspermum ammi*, an annual plant native to southern India, that is closely related to caraway and cumin. The scent and flavour is much like a rough-and-ready peppery thyme, with a pleasing hint of aniseed and an excellent pungent sharpness. It likes to be in the company of carbs, and is a great partner for flatbreads, pakoras, in pickles, and with fish. It is one of the flavours in Bombay mix.

Using
The seeds may seem mild to the nose, but a gentle pounding with a pestle and mortar releases their potency. Use sparingly to avoid overpowering bitterness. When cooked, the thyme elements of the flavour come through more notably. A gentle toasting in a dry pan enhances its flavour while easing back on the bitterness. Buy whole ajowan where possible.

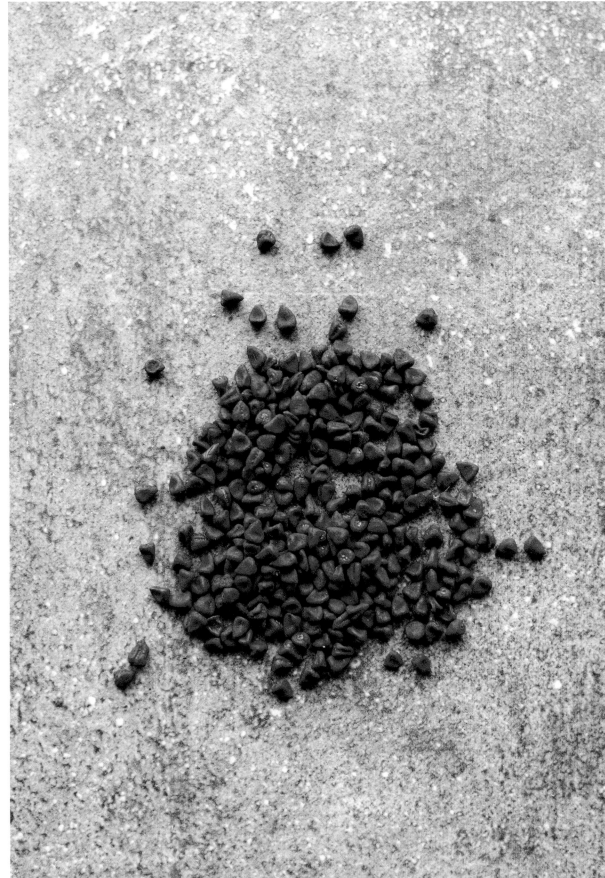

ALLSPICE

Blends

Baharat

Berbere

Jerk seasoning

Lebkuchengewürz

Mixed spice

Mulling spice

Ras el hanout

Affinities

Apples

Aubergine (eggplant)

Beef

Blackcurrants

Cabbage

Chicken

Dairy

Fish

Lamb

Pastry and cakes

Pineapple

Pork

Rhubarb

Rice

Root vegetables

Stone fruit

Sweet potato

Squash

Tomatoes

A warm, aromatic, sweet spice from an evergreen tree that is native to the Caribbean and central America, where the majority is still grown. Unsurprisingly, it features prominently in that region's cuisine. It shares a primary element – eugenol – with cloves, which provides part of this spice's intense coming together of clove, mace, bay, pepper and cinnamon flavours. The dried berries are large, and – as with most pepper – much of the flavour is in the outer shell, though the entire berry is commonly used.

Using

Buy whole allspice, and grind or gently crush it as you need it. Its ability to complement other spices makes it a distinctive, enhancing partner in very different spice blends. Cracking the whole berries and toasting in a dry pan over a low heat enhances the smoky elements of its flavour, and releases flavour compounds in the skin. That warm yet bright intensity and its natural preservative properties makes allspice excellent in pickling brines; the soused mackerel (page 136) shows it off perfectly. Lively sauces and spicy condiments often owe much to allspice: try the brown sauce (page 95) and kecap manis (page 94) for starters. Allspice's warming character flavours rice beautifully, as well as cakes and desserts – notably Christmas pudding – and it is an essential in mulled cider (page 264).

AMCHOOR

Made from unripe mangoes, this sun-dried powder has a full, sweet fruitiness alongside its citric sharpness, and is a wonderful way of souring soups and salads. Amchoor is widely used in northern India where the trees thrive, whereas tamarind is a more popular souring agent where it flourishes in the south.

Using

Widely available in powdered form, you may also find amchoor as dried slices: the powdered form keeps for up to a year in a sealed container, though once you have a taste for it you'll get through it much more quickly. As with anardana (below), amchoor is hugely versatile: use it to sour and flavour curries, stews, soups, to sprinkle on sweet and savoury – from panisse to pakoras, to cheesecake to rice pudding – and to flavour and tenderize meat prior to cooking. It is a crucial part of chaat masala, one of the greatest and most versatile spice blends. An excellent agent of acidity, it adds sourness without increasing the liquid in the recipe as using lemon does.

ANARDANA

I love pomegranate in all forms, including this beautifully sour, dried incarnation. Available in whole seed or powdered form, anardana is sharp, fruity and has a long tangy finish that is especially popular in northern Indian and Iranian cooking. Anardana from India and Pakistan is often made with wild pomegranate seeds, which are a little more bitter – not a downside in this context.

Using

As with amchoor (above), anardana is a wonderful souring agent – adding sharpness to curries, chutneys, stews and soups without increasing the liquid content. It is superb dusted on sweet or savoury dishes: try it on raita, cheesecake, barbecued buttered sweetcorn, flatbreads and panisse for starters.

ANISE SEED

Blends

Garam masala

Lebkuchengewürz

Ras el hanout

Affinities

Alcohol

Apples

Asparagus

Banana

Beef

Blackcurrants

Breads

Celeriac

Chestnuts

Chicken

Chocolate

Dairy

Figs

Fish

Garlic

Lamb

Lemon

Lentils

Nuts

Oily fish

Pastry, cakes and biscuits

Pineapple

Pork

Potatoes

Rhubarb

Root vegetables

Rye

Stone fruit

The old faux-rhetorical 'What have the Romans ever done for us?' has quite the stack of responses – public sanitation, high-quality transport networks and more; and to that I add that they embraced the pleasure of anise in food and drinks. The small, aromatic seeds of this eastern Mediterranean plant have a distinctive aniseed, liquorice flavour that's warm and gentle. While not containing sugar, the high proportion of anethole reads on the tongue as intensely sweet.

Using

It is perhaps most widely used in breads and sweet bakes (such as pan de muerto, page 111). It pairs beautifully with most fruit: the qalat daqqa plum cake (page 223) is so good with figs instead of plums and anise in the spice mix. That said, its affinity for lentils, lamb and pork – whether fried chops or slow-cooked stews – makes it hugely versatile. It has quite the pedigree in flavouring drinks: ouzo, arrack and pastis to name but three. Seeds retain their flavour for at least a year, but quickly lose it once ground. Anethole doesn't dissolve in water, so combine with alcohol or fat (gently fry the seeds in a little oil or butter) to increase its presence in a dish.

ASAFOETIDA

Blends
Chaat masala
Curry powder
Gunpowder mix

Affinities
Beans
Chicken
Fish
Lamb
Onions
Pulses
Root vegetables

Aka hing. It's hard to describe the pungent, rather grim scent of raw, powdered asafoetida in positive terms – think bitter, funky fermented garlic kept in your unfit brother's football sock – but heat and fat transform it, releasing a wonderful oniony garlic flavour. Harvested as gum resin from a species of Ferula of Central Asia, asafoetida is widely used throughout the region, and especially popular with those for whom garlic and onion are out of bounds for religious or intolerance reasons.

Using
Most widely available in solid or powdered form, asafoetida has a long shelf life, less so once ground. It is used widely in India in vegetable, meat and pulse dishes, usually added sparingly to bring distinctiveness to curries and dhals. It has a particular affinity for pastry and frying: pakoras use its magic well. It is an essential element of chaat masala.

CARDAMOM – BLACK

Blends
Advieh
Garam masala
Niter kibbeh
Ras al hanout

Affinities
Beef
Black pepper
Carrots
Cauliflower
Chocolate
Cinnamon
Clove
Coconut
Figs
Greens, especially
dark-leaved kales
Lamb
Lentils
Peas
Potatoes
Rice
Root vegetables
Tomatoes

Entirely different to the more widely used green cardamom, this is the seed of a few *Amomum* and *Aframomum* species, with *Amomum subulatum* – aka Nepal cardamom – the most notable. The seeds are picked and dried over an open fire; their scent and flavour is smoky, piney and a little camphorous, reminding me of my long-gone grandfather's pipe tobacco.

Black cardamom is used almost entirely in savoury recipes, often adding depth and earth to spice blends. It is one of the 'hot' spices – i.e. rather than being chilli-hot, it encourages the body to create warmth; it combines beautifully with others such as clove, cinnamon and black pepper in garam masala, which means 'hot spices'.

Using
The pods can be used whole or the seeds within extracted; these can be used whole or ground. The seeds have a long shelf life, but lose clarity and impact quickly when ground. Meat and rice were made for it: try it in a lamb biryani, allowed to infuse into steaming rice or as a component of garam masala. A little ground black cardamom dusted to serve on stews and roasted vegetables brings a smoky, meaty savouriness.

Pictured opposite.

CARDAMOM - GREEN

Native to southern India and Sri Lanka, cardamom is another of those delightful warm spices that works as well in savoury dishes as in sweet. Beautifully perfumed and distinctive in flavour, it is quite the ball of contradictions: bold but mellow, sweet yet citrusy, warm but fresh and clean, with camphor and smoke sitting in there somewhere. Used widely in Indian, Sri Lankan and Middle Eastern cooking, it reached northern Europe thanks to the Vikings, and is very much a part of Scandinavian cooking. The seeds within the papery pods carry the flavour.

Using

Hugely versatile, green cardamom is used in many types of curry (notably kormas, pilafs and biryanis), northern European biscuits, buns and cakes, in ice creams such as kulfi, in drinks as diverse as cardamom coffee (page 265), lassis and Seville orange gin. A good tweak added to the filling of a chocolate tart or brownie is greatly advised. Green pods are often a sign of good-quality cardamom: pale pods are likely to have been bleached. If you can, crack one open before you buy: a certain tackiness of the seeds indicates freshness. Extricate the seeds to use; the pods have little flavour and the texture isn't special.

CASSIA

Blends
Baharat
Chinese five-spice
Five-spice salt
Ras el hanout

Blends

Baharat

Chinese five-spice

Five-spice salt

Ras el hanout

Affinities

Apples

Aubergine (eggplant)

Beef

Chocolate

Chicken

Duck

Figs

Game

Lamb

Lentils

Pastry and cakes

Pork

Rice

Squash

Stone fruit

Sweet potato

Tomatoes

It is probable that the beautifully aromatic bark of the South East Asian cassia tree reached the Mediterranean before the similar cinnamon. Cassia has a reputation in some quarters as a coarse cinnamon: its higher levels of volatile oils mean it tends to be fuller in aroma and flavour; it is often sweeter, as well as harder to break down or grind to a powder than cinnamon. It also carries less eugenol and hence less clove-iness, as well as a little bitterness thanks to the tannins present. This isn't necessarily a bad thing.

Using

Perfect used whole in slow-cooked dishes such as curries, where its warm, bittersweet flavour can be released over time. Suits rich meats such as pheasant and duck a little more than cinnamon. A fine substitute for cinnamon in five-spice. I generally prefer cassia over cinnamon in ice creams, as its bolder presence helps compensate for the slightly dampening effect freezing has on flavours.

CARAWAY

For a spice not perhaps widely used, caraway has a very long history of appreciation; as far back as the Stone Age for sure. It was the Romans who did much to speed and popularize it, but it seems too little used these days. Let's put that to rights. These small seeds taste like a cross between cumin and thyme, with a nudge of orange peel, mint and aniseed – at once warm, comforting and refreshing.

Using
Classically used in sauerkraut, a variety of northern European breads (including pumpernickel and Serbian salty rolls) and desserts, as well as North African dishes: it is a characteristic ingredient of harissa (page 65). It brings depth and brightness to stews and soups, including goulash, and pairs superbly with most meats, especially fatty game and poultry. I love caraway added to a lemon/oil dressing for cooked cabbage. The shelf life is short compared to many spices, so buy in small amounts. Combine and/or warm with oil before using if you want the flavour to be carried in the recipe, rather than as punctuation when you eat the seed.

CELERY SEED

As with coriander, fennel and dill, celery produces a seed that carries the flavour of its parent, in this case much more prominently. Most celery seed is produced from wild celery rather than cultivars grown for vegetable production. Popular in the colder climates of northern Europe and beyond, as well as in India and surrounding countries, celery seed loves cold weather vegetables as much as sunny tomatoes. It has upfront bitterness that mellows with cooking, and there are gentler, grassy, earthy flavours of parsley and mace, as well as the brightness of citrus tucked in there too.

Using
Celery seed brings superb punctuation to pickles and other preserves, as well as when sprinkled over breads and fried savouries such as pakoras. It is strong, and a little goes a long way, hence it is often used in combination with salt to bring a little of its flavour while seasoning: try making a small batch, one part celery seed to four parts salt. It really helps a Bloody Mary along. An excellent pickling spice, celery seed also takes well to dairy and mayonnaise: a sprinkle in a coleslaw or remoulade dressing, or over a dauphinoise, is a real elevator.

CHILLI

Affinities

Almost everything

If any spice could fill a book, fat as you like, chilli is it. The variety, the breadth of flavours, intensities, fruitiness and impact of both dried and fresh is a song to culinary and horticultural diversity. Grown for millennia in its native Mexico and the Americas to its south, chillies came to Europe via Columbus in the late 1400s, spreading through colonies and trading to Asia and Africa. A few short centuries later, chillies are characteristic of the food of so many cultures.

Chillies split into two key groups, the vegetable chillies (various *Capsicum annuum* species) and spice chillies (*Capsicum chinense*). Vegetable chillies tend to be thick-fleshed and large-fruited, and are usually fairly mild: Hungarian Hot Wax is widely available. Pimiento de Padrón is a favourite of the classic Russian roulette Spanish tapas: picked young and tender, it is usually very mild and delicious, with the occasional hot rogue. Spice chillies are largely thin-fleshed and small-fruited, usually fairly to very hot. Excellent fresh, they also dry very well. Habaneros belong to the spice chillies. While they include many varieties, including Scotch bonnets, the habanero's unifying characteristic is a full fruitiness.

It is usual for chillies to mature to somewhere along the spectrum from green through yellows, oranges and reds and occasionally to purples and black; dried chillies are almost always left to ripen to red, hence the colour of most chilli powder.

Using

As with pepper, there is almost nothing which chilli fails to enhance. When a chilli is dried, the ratio of capsaicin to chilli weight increases: the chilli heat intensifies. Capsaicin is the key compound that delivers the heat: in the hotter chillies it can overpower the most subtle characteristics – the fruitiness of habaneros, for example. It is generated in the white inner pith, so removing this is the fastest way of reducing the heat. Choosing whether to use fresh, ground or flakes of chilli is very much down to personal preference. Of the many varieties available, a small selection of favourites below.

Urfa chilli, aka isot biber – a very dark, mild Turkish chilli with a warm, gentle, smoky flavour, carrying a dash of citrus and raisin to it. The ripe fruit are sun-dried by day and bound together to ferment at night to intensify their flavour, before being reduced to powder or flakes; widely used in Turkish cooking. Really good in a brownie.

Guajillo – a dark, sweet, dried, smoky vegetable chilli with gentle to medium heat. A Mexican favourite. Superb with fish, in pastes and sauces and one I love to sprinkle flakes of over soups, flatbreads and roasted squash.

Ancho – a roasted, dried poblano, popular in Mexican cooking, available as whole, flakes or powder. Their flavour is very mild, of rich, raisiny tobacco, with a sweet fruitiness. They work particularly well in a mole (page 137), or stuffed. It goes well with pork, chicken, most vegetables and wonderfully with chocolate.

Pasilla – slightly hotter than many chillies used in Mexico, this long slender chilli is a dried chilaca, with a sweet liquorice, fruity flavour with hints of cocoa.

Aleppo pepper, aka pul biber – a popular Syrian/Turkish chilli most commonly available as flakes. This is my go-to default sprinkle chilli: it adds a little bite, plenty of colour and fruitiness. Classically added to doner kebabs.

Piquín – a tiny red Mexican chilli with a fruity, smoky flavour and plenty of heat. Go easy: this is for hot sauces and oils where you want a serious kick.

Scotch bonnet – one of the habaneros, full of fruitiness and often very hot. Widely used fresh and dried, and a favourite of Caribbean cooking.

Kashmiri – usually available as a vibrant red powder and flakes from these short oval chillies. Mild but full-flavoured, excellent in tandoori dishes, with fish and in curries.

Gochugaru, aka Korean red pepper powder – a sweet, bright yet smoky, fruity chilli with lively heat. Available in various grades of powder and flakes. An essential ingredient of kimchi, but suits so many other recipes.

Chipotle – smoke-dried jalapeños, with a beautifully rich, chocolatey sweetness. Often used split to flavour a dish, then removed, or ground to a powder for more intensity. Use dried or rehydrate (see Note below).

Cayenne – almost always dried. Intense in flavour and colour. Bright and direct, important to South and North American cuisine, as well as Indian cooking. Used commonly in hot sauces, with seafood and in lentil dishes where dry heat is required. The choice when devilling kidneys or eggs.

Naga jolokia and Carolina Reaper – insanely hot chillies that can easily exceed 40,000 times more heat than a mild vegetable chilli. Can bring serious discomfort: I wouldn't even look at them too long if I were you.

Note:
To use whole dried chillies, add as they are to long-cooked dishes. For more intense flavour or if shorter cooking time: wipe clean, slit along a long side with a sharp knife, open out and remove seeds and the stem end; toast in a dry pan over a low–medium heat, cover in just-boiled water and allow to rehydrate for 10–15 minutes. Then add as is, chopped or whizzed to a paste.

CINNAMON

Cinnamon's early traders guarded its origin closely: it was harvested from an unknown land by giant birds who built their clifftop nests with its fragrant sticks, in turn collected by those brave enough to distract the fearsome creatures with slaughtered oxen. When the Portuguese rumbled the ruse in the 16th century by finding cinnamon trees in their native Sri Lanka, it inspired them to colonize the island before the Dutch moved in for a piece of the action. Today, you can wander to the shops in search of cinnamon without fear of much more than someone vigorously shaking a charity box at you.

Cinnamon is from the bark of young shoots of the cinnamon tree, peeled and laid in layers like filo, and rolled into long aromatic cigars known as quills. It brings warmth and comfort – it feels like home when winter is harsh – and is rarely unwelcome. While intense, cinnamon remains gentle, and while not sweet itself, it implies it by enhancing other ingredients to give that effect. A key compound – cinnamaldehyde – reads as warming on the tongue, and is a component of garam masala (page 64): cinnamaldehyde doesn't dissolve in water, but fats and alcohol carry this element of its flavour well. Cinnamon suits savoury and sweet recipes equally, and is one of the most widely used spices, adding warmth to North American and Scandinavian breads, North African tagines and soups, and Catalan desserts, among so many others.

Using

Cinnamon is classified into grades that indicate its quality, not that most of us would know it: counter-intuitively perhaps, the thinner, paler quills are often the finest; if you buy ground cinnamon, the palest is often best. Ground cinnamon loses its punch relatively quickly – it smells grand, but delivers less on the tongue. Use quickly or grind fresh from sticks. Use the finest quality cinnamon where its subtleties won't get lost – so rice pudding rather than tagine, etc. Adding cinnamon early in the cooking process gives it time to release its flavour fully: which is not to say a dash of ground cinnamon over a dessert or hot chocolate isn't to be encouraged. Try stirring your coffee with a cinnamon stick, as you may find people doing in Mexico. And if breakfast could do with a sweetening, you'll be after the cinnamon sugar on page 62.

CINNAMON BERRIES

Blends

Lebkuchengewürz

Mixed spice

Mulled spice

Sweet dukkah

Affinities

Apples

Aubergine (eggplant)

Chocolate

Cider

Lamb

Lentils

Liver

Melon

Stone fruit

Wine

Originating from China, these berries are not widely available but they really should be sought out: they carry a potent floral scent and flavour of cinnamon, orange zest and pepper. As unfamiliar as it may be to some, cinnamon berries have a long medicinal and culinary history.

Using

Cinnamon berries can happily be substituted for a slightly different impression where cassia or cinnamon sticks are used (try a few in the Lebkuchengewürz blend, page 67), added to mulled drinks (especially cider, page 264), pickles and marinades. A great substitution for cinnamon in mixed spice.

CLOVES

Cloves are the sun-dried flower buds from a tropical evergreen tree native to Indonesia. The top of the 'club' is the unopened petals of the flower buds that are picked twice a year, when red/pink, just ahead of opening. Cloves are remarkable and intense: they have the highest eugenol content of any spice, giving them a flavour that's warm, camphorous, peppery, fruity and full-on, as well as bringing implied sweetness to other ingredients. Cloves are such the essence of Christmas that it is perfectly usual for it to appear in many of the elements of a British Christmas dinner: including studding the onions in the bread sauce, in the festive ham, as well as spicing the Christmas pudding and mince pies.

Using

The best cloves should be plump, intact, and slightly oily when pressed. Fat and alcohol carry their flavour well, and as a rule it's best to add them early to allow their flavour to be released slowly. Cloves can easily dominate, hence often used sparingly and/or in combination with other warming spices – often cinnamon and/or fennel. Superb with dairy, in desserts, studded in ham, used to flavour red cabbage and other braises, in pickles and sauces. Once its flavour has been imparted the clove itself is often discarded. One of the 'hot' spices essential to garam masala.

CORIANDER SEED

Blends
Advieh

Baharat

Berbere

Bumbu paste

Cape Malay spice blend

Chaat masala

Chimichurri

Dukkah

Durban curry powder

Garam masala

Gunpowder mix

Harissa

Hawaij

Khmeli-suneli

Mixed spice

Niter kibbeh

Ras el hanout

Sajji masala

Svanuri marili

Sri Lankan curry powder

Sweet dukkah

Tempero baiano

Zhug

Affinities
Apples and pears

Aubergine (eggplant)

Beer

Blueberries

Cabbage

Cauliflower

Celery

Chicken

Citrus

Coffee

Fish and shellfish

Game

Goat's cheese

Ham

Lamb

Mushrooms

Oats

Olives

Onions

Pork

Potatoes

Pulses

Stone fruit

Tomatoes

I sometimes forget that coriander (cilantro) leaf and seed are from the same plant, even though I grow it for both in the garden. The leaves are bright, fresh, lush and generally added to serve, whereas the seeds (botanically actually a fruit, containing two seeds) bring warmth, depth and can take long or harsh cooking: happily, there are endless recipes where their complementary flavours work together perfectly. The flavour and scent of dried coriander is light and mild but clear: orange zest, pepper, gently resinous and floral. It seems to have made the journey from the eastern Mediterranean to India and its neighbours as BCE became CE, and in the centuries that followed through China and to Western Europe, from where settlers introduced it to the Americas. It has become a two-harvests-for-one-plant favourite the world over. Growing coriander for seed allows you the luxury of fresh green seed; not better than dried coriander, but carrying a mellow floralness that is different to the dried spice.

Using
Buying whole seed allows you to choose the grade of the grinding (or not to grind them at all) and gives a fresher flavour when ground as you need it. Sitting not too far into the earthy or pungent, coriander finds its way into many spice blends, and works surprisingly well with fruit and sweet recipes (such as cakes and biscuits), as well as in pickles. Coriander works particularly well with olives: a few days infusing in olive oil with crushed coriander seed and lemon zest transforms even ordinary olives. And you must try the shortbread on page 217 with coriander instead of the wattleseed. Where coriander is to be used as a primary ingredient (such as the clafoutis on page 213) and undiluted by spicy partners, it is really worth using Indian coriander – an oval-seeded upgrade in quality and sweetness from that widely available. A gentle toasting in a dry pan develops its flavour.

CUMIN

Cumin is the seed of a relatively unimpressive small plant native of the Nile valley but widely grown where the sun shines hot. It is one of the cornerstones of Indian cooking and is also widely used in many other cultures as diverse as Mexican, Dutch and North African. Deeply musty and woody in scent – it reminds me of jumble sale suits – it pairs beautifully with many other spices. I suspect that with the exception of pepper, I use cumin – on its own or in blends – more than any other spice.

Using

Perhaps more than any other, cumin benefits from gentle dry-roasting in a frying pan just prior to using – a sweet nuttiness comes to the fore. Cumin is among the most well-travelled and loved spices, adding depth to curries, chutneys, pulse recipes including falafel and so much more. Its ability to pair with other spices is almost unsurpassed: used with coriander it underlies much of India's food, and is a characteristic element of so many spice blends and pastes. As much as cumin is known – rightly – as a fine accompaniment to lamb, it works equally well dusted over pork chops prior to cooking. Black cumin seeds are smaller, a touch more musty and thymey, and very good. Seeds will keep flavour locked up for months, but once ground its qualities fade rapidly.

DILL SEED

Blends
Khmeli-suneli
Svanuri marili

Affinities
Apples
Aubergine (eggplant)
Beans
Beef
Bread
Cabbage
Carrots
Cauliflower
Citrus
Courgette (zucchini)
Cucumber
Dairy
Eggs
Fish
Lamb
Onions
Potatoes
Rice
Root vegetables
Seafood
Spinach
Squash
Vinegar

Dill seed comes from a small, rather beautiful plant that originates from where Asia, Europe and Russia meet. As with coriander, fennel and so on, it gives us a leafy herb and later the seeds that carry the similar flavour and scent. Thanks to the chemical carvone they share, there is much in common between caraway and dill seed, though dill comes with soft aniseed and parsley notes.

Using
Dill seed pairs with acidity beautifully, and is widely used in pickling and curing. Indian dill – a slight variation on the common variety – produces slightly larger seed, with a more pronounced flavour, and offers more impact in curries, slow-cooked stews, soups and pickle blends. Whole seeds have a shelf life of in excess of a year, but the flavour quickly declines once ground. A gentle toasting in a dry pan works very well at bringing complexity to dill's flavour. Long cooking gives a mellow impact, a late dusting much brighter. I find it especially good added to carrot and cauliflower before roasting, with a light sprinkle to serve, and dusted generously into melted butter to dress the first potatoes of the season.

DRIED LIMES

Blends

Baharat

Chaat masala

Sour chilli seasoning

Affinities

Beans

Chicken

Chickpeas

Couscous

Fish

Fruit

Grains

Lamb

Lentils

Rice

Vegetables

Also known as Persian limes, dried limes are made by brining and sun-drying ripe, green limes; forming hard, feather-light, honeycomb globes. White dried limes, with a beautiful sour, citrus flavour are produced; those left to dry longer darken into black limes, and typically have a stronger, earthy, richer flavour. Dried limes are especially good as a souring agent in sours and stews.

Using

Available as powder or whole; whole limes are punctured and added to dishes to infuse. Long cooking – classically in curries and stews, such as the Iranian khoresht – allows more flavour to be released, but some top notes can be lost, so add a little dusting of ground lime to serve if that suits. I particularly love dried limes in fish curries. Crushed, they make refreshing sour drinks (page 244), rubs for meat and sprinkling on soups, lentils dishes and salads. Try a couple, cracked, in basmati rice as it cooks.

ETHIOPIAN PASSION BERRIES

Blends

Berbere

Mulled spice

Sweet dukkah

Affinities

Apples

Chicken

Chocolate

Cider

Dairy

Fish

Pears

Stone fruit

The first time I smelled passion berries, I drifted off a little. For a few seconds I was gone, like the first time I heard Spirit of Eden. My mind filled with a cascade of what-abouts; where it might work, with what it might chime. I've yet to run out of ideas, and neither will you. As you might hope, these small olive-coloured dried berries are heady with the sweet full scent of passion fruit. The flavour carries much of that, as well as a gentle but present pepperiness.

Using

Perhaps surprisingly given their upfront passion fruit flavour, passion berries work as well in savoury recipes as they do sweet. They are essential in Ethiopia's national dish, doro wat (page 182), and – in the same way cinnamon can – they complement baked fish or lamb dishes. Ground, they add zing and impact to poached or baked fruit and creamy desserts: you have to make the Ethiopian passion berry and tonka bean ice cream (page 231). Try a dusting on the trifle (page 234) or the tarte tatin (page 206) too.

Pictured opposite.

FENNEL

Native to the Mediterranean, fennel seed is used from both wild and cultivated forms of this umbelliferous plant; the seeds' sweet aniseed flavour is similar to fennel leaf but stronger, with the cultivated form often sweeter than the wild. Its flavour can be peculiarly cool and refreshing, and/or warm and comforting, depending how deployed. What we buy as fennel seed is actually the fruit, inside which are seeds, but only a dullard would point that out.

Using

Fennel is widely used in savoury recipes – including salamis, five-spice, panch phoran – as well as desserts and sweet bakes such as crumbles, shortbread and other biscuits, and is a key component of spice blends throughout Europe and Asia. Fennel complements most meats, though perhaps most particularly pork: try the chorizo and merguez mixes on page 153, which are as good for meatballs as they are for Scotch eggs. Fennel benefits from a little light toasting in a dry pan, bringing nuttiness along with the sweetness, or as one of the spices in a tadka, fried in oil to release the flavours before adding to serve. Even if you are not grinding the seeds to a powder, a little attention from the mortar and pestle helps release the oils held just beneath the surface of the ridges and draw out more of that flavour.

FENUGREEK

Blends

Berbere

Cape Malay spice blend

Durban curry powder

Gunpowder mix

Khmeli-suneli

Niter kibbeh

Panch phoran

Svanuri marili

Affinities

Beef

Bread

Fish

Lamb

Lentils

Potatoes

Squash

Sweet potato

Walnuts

Originating from where south-eastern Europe meets Asia, fenugreek's mustard-coloured, pyramidal seeds have a bold, deliciously bitter curry scent and sweet-bitter, syrup-coffee, lovage-like flavour that is used widely in Indian, West African and Iranian cooking. I find its scent and flavour reach a little savoury corner of my soul that nothing else quite touches. Blue fenugreek is a milder, less bitter incarnation which is native to and popular in Georgia.

Using

A light toasting in a dry pan brings their smoky nuttiness to the fore; too long accentuates their bitterness. Fenugreek has a long shelf life: grind seeds as you need them as their qualities fade quickly after. The diversity of spice blends of which it is a part attest to its versatility: a little toasted, crushed and added to stews and lentil dishes brings a deep underlying savouriness. Blue fenugreek is an essential element of khmeli-suneli – a Georgian spice blend that is such a satisfying finishing sprinkle to stews, soups and pretty much anything that's been roasted.

GINGER

Dried ginger has quite a different culinary history to its fresh incarnation, as its dried form reached distant cultures far ahead of its fresh. Their flavours are only so similar: while they share a woody hotness, dried ginger is more pungent and hot, and a touch less citrusy.

Using

As well as being lively and warm when used solo – especially with apples and squash – ginger is perhaps most appreciated in combination with other spices, where its distinctiveness occupies a place in the spice continuum that draws together others – as different as pepper, cumin and star anise – into gentler blends such as quatre épices, or more intense such as advieh. As with cinnamon, ginger is at home in savoury as sweet, being part of curry blends and tagines, as well as biscuit and dessert recipes.

GRAINS OF PARADISE

Blends
Qalat daqqa

Ras el hanout

Affinities
Apples

Aubergine (eggplant)

Chicken

Citrus

Fish

Lamb

Potatoes

Rice

Root vegetables

Squash

Stone fruit

Strawberries

Sweet potato

Tomatoes

A tall ginger-like perennial native to the tropical west coast of Africa provides us with seeds in the form of grains of paradise, a fruity, gingery, peppery, warm spice that has many similarities with pepper. It goes by a number of akas, including Guinea pepper and alligator pepper, though it is actually a close relative of the latter rather than the same. It was used as a pepper substitute for some time, having reached Europe 900 years ago, but as pepper became more readily available, use of grains of paradise greatly reduced. However, in western and North Africa, grains of paradise remain as popular as ever, where it is commonly used to flavour stews, soups and rice dishes.

Using
Grains of paradise has a fragrant pepperiness that works well with many fruit; strawberries and plums especially. Cooking with oil or another fat releases the flavour well. Adding it late to dishes keeps the flavour most apparent, though it makes an excellent component of a rub for meat prior to cooking. Most commonly used crushed or ground: as a powder it loses intensity quickly.

JUNIPER

Affinities
Alcohol

Apple

Beef

Beetroot (beet)

Blackcurrants

Cabbage

Chicken

Chocolate

Citrus

Duck

Fish – especially salmon

Goose

Lamb

Olives

Pork

Rabbit

Rye

Venison

Vodka

Juniper is a small, prickly, evergreen tree of the cypress family that grows across many of the chalky uplands of the northern hemisphere. Its berries are beautifully bittersweet, citrusy, piney and aromatic: Pavlov's dog has me unable to separate its flavour and scent from its delightful influence on gin. Almost always available as whole dried – though softish – berries, juniper is most commonly used throughout the cooler countries in which it grows.

Using
Juniper is often used to complement fatty meats, especially game. Its characteristic flavour works really well with sourness – in particular in sauerkraut, in brines and pickling liquids (pages 77 and 84) – as well as chopped in pastes, pâtés, marinades and rubs for meat. If you are a fan of slow-cooked red cabbage at Christmas, try a few crushed juniper berries added halfway through. Branches make fine wood for smoking fish, meat and cheese. Lightly squish the berries to release their flavour more readily.

KOKUM

Kokum is the beautifully sour dried fruit of a tree from the mangosteen family, native to India. Though kokum is milder, it is used to acidify recipes in much the same way tamarind is in southern India and amchoor is to the north. It carries a peculiar flavour with hints of dried apricots and fermented apples, a distant saltiness (salt is often used in the drying process), and a characteristic sourness.

Using

Kokum is often used as a flavouring by soaking it in hot water, leaching its flavour into the liquid as it rehydrates; a good squeeze will encourage maximum flavour from it. This sour liquid is either used as is to brighten soups, stews and curries, or flavoured with garlic, ginger and other spices before using. Sol khadi, a spice-heavy drink popular on India's west coast, has kokum at its heart (page 246).

MAHLEB

As with most cherries, the mahleb cherry has a small stone at the centre of the fruit; unlike most cherries, mahleb stones are extraordinary, tasting of sweet rich cherries, almond and a soft woodiness. Crushing adds a hint of agreeable bitterness. Native to where Europe and Asia come together, mahleb has a long culinary history that is largely (and peculiarly) limited to its home patch and North Africa; I am busy trying to widen it.

Using

Mahleb is a spice for baking rather than dusting, its sweet flavours suiting cakes and biscuits particularly well. Cooking dials back the bitterness and brings the fruitiness to the fore: do try Honey & Co.'s phenomenal baklava (page 232). A few crushed kernels are delicious in sweet pastry, crumble topping and in combination with other spices as a rub for meat prior to cooking. Buy whole kernels if you can, or ground mahleb in small quantities, as its high oil content causes it to turn rancid in a relatively short time.

MUSTARD

Mustard is the seed from various brassica species, cultivated and naturalized widely. There are three common forms: yellow/white, brown and black. While the seeds are almost aromaless, crushing and the addition of water releases their heat and pungency; yellow/white are the mildest, black the largest and most intense, with brown the middle ground but with the longest-lasting flavour. Combinations are used to create widely used mustards in powdered and sauce form. They span the spectrum, from lively and hot English mustard (using brown and yellow/white seeds), to the gentle subtlety of Dijon mustard. Regional variations are many: the Dutch Zwolle mustard incorporates dill seed, many American mustards include a little turmeric for colour and flavour, and English mustard often comes with excellent nasal clearing effects, perfect with steaks and ham in particular.

Using
The paler seeds are superb in pickles (such as piccalilli, page 83). The isothiocyanates that bring pungency are released when the seeds are soaked or split open, hence smelling or sucking mustard seeds offers little. The brown seeds are commonly used in Indian cookery, in mustard oil, curry pastes and for tadkas where frying in oil activates elements of their flavour without the (often welcome, sometimes not) pungency that comes with the addition of water. Mustard is central to the classic Italian condiment mostarda di frutta (page 102), flavouring the syrup in which the fruit are simmered and preserved. Mustards in powdered or sauce form are widely used in dressings (such as the classic vinaigrette) and marinades and pastes.

NUTMEG AND MACE

Blends

Baharat

Berbere

Bumbu paste

Garam masala

Jerk seasoning

Lebkuchengewürz

Mixed spice

Niter kibbeh

Qalat daqqa

Quatre épices

Ras el hanout

Sweet garam masala

Affinities

Apple

Aubergine (eggplant)

Cabbage

Carrot

Cauliflower

Celery

Cheese

Chicken

Dairy

Eggs

Fish

Honey

Lamb

Liver

Onion

Pastry and cakes

Pork

Potato

Seafood

Spinach

Squash

Stone fruit

Sweet potato

Myristica fragrans is an evergreen tree native to Indonesia, with a gorgeous-looking fruit somewhere between an apricot and a small pear. A single tree can produce 10,000 fruit a year. Inside each, the prize: the single oval seed provides us with nutmeg, its cycle-helmet wrapper (known as an aril) gives us mace. Once picked, the seed is soaked in water, and the mace outer casing is flattened and, along with the nutmeg, allowed to dry. They have similar scent and flavour – warm, comforting, sweet, woody, faintly of orange, lemon, clove and mild pepper – with mace less astringent, and nutmeg more piney. So prized and travelled are mace and nutmeg that one or both finds itself in spice blends as diverse as Tunisia's qalat daqqa and Jamaica's jerk seasoning.

Using

Mace is available in three common forms: semi-intact lanterns, lanterns broken into slender ribs known as blades, and ground. Nutmeg is one of the longer-lasting spices: the scent is released by an enthusiastic coming together with a mini grater. Buy it whole rather than ground. Both are widely used in sweet and savoury recipes, from rice puddings to garam masala, to season meat dishes of many cultures, including the UK where it is commonly found in haggis, pâtés, potted seafood (page 116) and pie recipes. Fragrant, delicate yet also robust enough to persist in the presence of heat, nutmeg and mace are the bringers of comfort and a sense of Sunday afternoons. Where dairy is present, nutmeg and mace complement: béchamel sauce, rice pudding, custard, ricotta and more, all benefit from their charm. They may not be the loudest in the choir, but their voice is sweet. Where nutmeg or mace are the main flavouring – e.g. atop rice pudding – I tend to add it late as the flavours can be lost with too much cooking. I use mace where I want less attack than nutmeg and more of the floral, as well as length of flavour.

NIGELLA

Blends
Panch phoran

Affinities
Bread
Chicken
Dairy
Eggs
Lamb
Leafy greens
Pastry
Potato
Pulses
Rice
Root vegetables
Squash

These little angular seeds from *Nigella sativa* – a blue-flowered annual native to the eastern Mediterranean and the Middle East – add an earthy flavour like peppery, slightly burnt onions cooked with oregano. Their flavour is released with heat and crushing, and they are commonly used in North African and Indian breads, curries and pickles.

Using
So good is nigella sprinkled on lightly oiled flatbreads and pastries that it is tempting to use it only for that; the spice blend panch phoran is the antidote to that urge. The raita on page 88 is differently excellent with nigella instead of the mustard seeds. Avoid ground nigella: whole seeds keep much longer and the flavour is better. Grind them in an electric grinder as a combination of size and hardness makes them unsuitable for the pestle and mortar.

PAPRIKA

Blends
Berbere
Blackening seasoning
Chimichurri
Jerk seasoning
Ras el hanout
Tempero baiano

Affinities
Beef
Chicken
Couscous
Duck
Eggs
Lamb
Melon
Noodles
Offal
Onion
Pineapple
Plum
Pork
Potato
Pulses
Rice
Root vegetables
Seafood
Venison
Walnuts

I might well have put paprika in the loving embrace of the chilli section (page 29) but despite it being made from dried chillies of the *Capsicum annuum* species to which many mild, fleshy chillies belong, it has very much its own culinary identity. Widely available in hot and smoked forms, both are dried, powdered peppers, with hardwood smoke – often oak – used to create the smoked version. While its scent is gently fruity (and perhaps smoky), the flavour is alert and poky, pungent and bitter, with varying degrees of sweetness. Columbus brought peppers to Spain from the Americas in the late 15th century, hence a long history of paprika in Spanish cooking. Chilli intensity varies considerably, as paprika can be made from chillies of all heats: Hungarian paprika tends to be made from hotter varieties than in Spain or the USA.

Using
Paprika varies in heat, smokiness, sweetness and impact: how and which to use depends very much on your and the recipe's intentions. A little of the highest quality, gentle Spanish paprika (see José Pizarro's pan-fried chicken on page 180) can make as much difference as the beautifully present hit of Hungarian paprika in a goulash. So versatile and well-travelled is paprika, you will find it used almost everywhere: in Morocco in tagines, Spain in paella, India for colour as much as flavour, and so on. Try a little mixed with salt and dusted over melon (page 104), over a potato salad, or chopped eggs. Avoid heating in a dry pan as paprika can burn easily.

PEPPER

Affinities

Pretty much anything

It is crazy in so many ways to try to cast all pepper into the shade of a single umbrella, but in many ways this is what many of us do daily: we shorthand the width of flavours and depth of aromas that the diverse world of pepper offers into a single representative: black pepper. Even with its almost daily use in many homes we seek supermarket mediocrity – let us raise our eyes a little higher than the perfectly reasonable. There are two areas to investigate: quality and variety. Buying whole peppercorns is almost always the shortest cut to an uplift in flavour and scent; using specialists who source quality pepper (see page 266) takes this to another level. Be inquisitive about varieties: Tellicherry pepper is extraordinary, Sarawak white pepper a jump so far up the ladder of pleasure from supermarket white pepper as to be almost laughable, and so on. A few moments of nosiness, and a small financial investment, are the only obstruction to reward. Pepper is as much experience as it is flavour and aroma. There's a woody fruitiness, varying degrees of citrus and heat; some species numb the lips and tongue, but it is undeniably a sensation.

Using

Piper nigrum, a vine native to southern India, produces peppercorns which have been long prized and much fought over. From this plant come four types of pepper. The underripe berries are picked as green pepper, which is typically fairly mild. At this point, they can be blanched, and allowed to darken and dry to be sold as black pepper; white pepper has been fermented then stripped of its outer coating, resulting in a bolder liveliness; left unpicked the peppercorns ripen fully to become pink pepper. Of the many pepper varieties available, a small selection of favourites below.

Sichuan pepper – a catch-all for a number of *Zanthoxylum* species that share a bright citrus pepperiness, along with the peculiarly addictive numbing it brings to the lips and tongue. The flavour is carried in the outer shell; hence it is often sold as half open, empty shells of flavour. It is an essential in five-spice and more widely used to contribute to the mala (page 167) so important to Sichuan cooking.

Sansho pepper, aka Japanese pepper – closely related to Sichuan pepper, yet considerably milder, with a creamier scent and flavour; it being less intense allows the aromatics to come more to the fore. Central to schichimi togarashi (page 70).

Nepalese pepper, aka Timur berry – of the same family as Sichuan and sansho peppers, this variety is heavily floral and grapefruity, which lends itself beautifully to seafood and fruit, especially strawberries.

Cubeb, aka tailed pepper or Indonesian pepper – this pepper carries an unusual, delicious mix of eucalyptus, clove, nutmeg and warm pepperiness that works especially well with lamb, game and other fatty foods. It's quite something with stone fruit, especially plums and peaches. It is an occasional – though to my mind all but essential – part of ras el hanout (page 69) where the nutmeg and eucalyptus flavours tie into the other spices perfectly.

Voatsiperifery pepper – closely related to the familiar pepper species of India, this superb fruity, floral and brightly citrus pepper is harvested in small quantities from the rainforests of Madagascar. It is rightly prized. Use where its character won't be lost by long cooking: dusted across a grilled fish, over scallops, over chocolate tarts or the best of summer's strawberries.

Long pepper – an Indonesian pepper with long catkin-like fruit with a bold peppery flavour with chocolate and cinnamon. It is equally suited to savoury and sweet: tagine and spaghetti sauces, in lentil dishes, sprinkled over grilled fish, ground over a crumble topping and enlivening long pepper cream (page 226) are just a few places I recommend its deployment.

Pink pepper – native of the South American Andes and unrelated to black pepper, the fruit are available dried or pickled, with a flavour that's fruity and piney, and easily lost next to more potent peppers. Perhaps best ground on strawberries or added to a simple lemon juice and olive oil dressing where its subtleties aren't lost.

For a shift in quality when it comes to black or white pepper, look for a PGI status (Protected Geographical Indication) that indicates quality and specificity of production. Sarawak white and black peppercorns are an excellent place to start. Tellicherry black pepper, from the coast of southern India, is an intense, complex yet bright upgrade on the usual. Similarly, Cambodia's rich and intense Kampot pepper is robust enough to accompany beef yet complex and restrained so as to not drive a bus over delicate fish. The rare white Penja pepper of Cameroon might be calmer than many white peppers but it brings a creamy, aromatic full-flavoured punch that works perfectly in mashed potato, in salami and on dark greens such as kale.

POPPY

Blends
Gunpowder mix

Affinities
Aubergine (eggplant)
Beans
Bread
Cauliflower
Citrus
Courgette (zucchini)
Fish
Honey
Onion
Pastry and cakes
Potato
Root vegetables
Yoghurt

Seeds of the opium poppy: what you lose in narcotic properties as they ripen you gain in nutty, almond flavour and scent for the kitchen. There are light and dark varieties: the light (commonly used in India) are gentle in flavour and scent, while dark (more familiar in Europe) are more intense and nuttier.

Using
Poppy seeds are familiar to many from their ubiquitous use on bagels and pretzels, where their nutty punctuation is entirely welcome. Combined with sugar and/or honey they are wonderful in sweet recipes such as halva and strudels. I confess never to have done this, but when poppy seeds – the white varieties especially – are ground they thicken as well as impart flavour to curries and stews. Dry-fry before using to accentuate their flavour. Buy in small amounts and store in an airtight container out of direct sunlight: poppy seeds' high oil content gives them a short shelf life.

SAFFRON

Blends
Ras el hanout

Affinities
Carrot
Chicken
Dairy
Eggs
Fish
Lamb
Leek
Lemon
Nuts
Pear
Potato
Rabbit
Rice
Root vegetables
Seafood
Spinach
Squash
Stone fruit
Tomato

Saffron has a highly unusual scent and flavour: an exquisite mix of just-cut hay and iron filings that's musky, bitter, smoky and honeyed; there are hints of the seaside to it too. It is expensive on account of both the unusualness of its flavour and that each of the three delicate stigmas of the particular species of crocus that give us saffron must be harvested by hand. Thankfully, little is needed to impart its wonderful red-amber colour and that magical flavour. Saffron is native to Iran and its neighbours and is classically found in sweet and savoury dishes of that region, and having travelled widely it can be found in Spanish and Scandinavian cakes, in Catalan paella, Cornish saffron bread, northern Italian risottos, Indian biryanis and the bouillabaisse of Mediterranean France.

Using
The deepest red indicates finer quality; that said, a few lighter shades are found in very good saffron. It imparts colour as well as flavour: the earlier it is added, the more of this it gives but at the expense of the fragile aroma which long cooking dissipates. Generally, saffron should be used sparingly as it is both intense and lingering. Steeping in water or oil releases both flavour and that sunset colour. Fish and seafood are such good partners for saffron: it is all but an essential in a fish soup. Saffron also has a great affinity with dairy: whisk saffron-infused milk into mashed potatoes, or into custard, and do try the ice cream on page 227.

STAR ANISE

Blends

Chinese five-spice

Five-spice salt

Garam masala

Mulled spice

Affinities

Apple

Banana

Beef

Bulb fennel

Cabbage and other greens

Chicken

Chocolate

Citrus

Duck

Figs

Leek

Pear

Pineapple

Pork

Rhubarb

Rice

Root vegetables

Seafood

Soy

Squash

Stone fruit

Sweet potato

The dried fruit of the Chinese magnolia tree gives us this gorgeous, comforting spice that brings sweetness and warmth wherever it's used. Somehow, its brand of aniseed-liquorice avoids the coolness of fennel or Korean mint, and is one of the key ingredients in Chinese five-spice and appears in some garam masala blends. Although sweet and aromatic, it complements so much that is savoury, including Vietnamese soups, Chinese stir fries and Keralan curries. It is, as the name implies, a sheriff's badge in form, with each of its eight spokes – known as carpels – containing small, shiny seeds.

Using

Much of star anise's flavour and scent is held in the carpels rather than the seeds: a dry-toasting, warming in alcohol or oil, or slow-cooking are all effective in encouraging the flavour out. As with bay, unless it's ground to a powder, it is used to infuse rather than be eaten. As much as it works beautifully with chicken, pork and as part of five-spice, it excels with fruit, especially apples, pears and plums. Other than in exceptional circumstances, it is a dereliction of your duties as a civilized human to omit star anise when mulling apple juice or cider. Star anise retains much of its flavour and scent for months in a sealed container, but quickly loses them once ground.

SUMAC

Blends

Za'atar

Affinities

Aubergine (eggplant)
Bread
Chicken
Chickpeas
Chips
Dairy
Fish
Hummus
Lamb
Pine nuts
Rice
Root vegetables
Seafood
Stone fruit
Yoghurt

The deep burgundy-red berries of the sumac bush are dried and crushed to produce this delightfully sour spice that's used throughout the Middle East (where it grows commonly) and beyond. It doesn't smell of a whole lot – a distant diesel spill perhaps – but it has a sharp, woody, fruity flavour that sits as well with a hot salty chip as it does with roasted plums.

Using

Before lemons arrived in Europe, the Romans used sumac for sourness; add it where you might otherwise employ lemon, tamarind, vinegar or dried lime. I particularly like sumac with fish as a rub or sprinkled on to serve. It has an ability to enhance flavours – a bit like salt does: I can't think of a better example of this than the bread salad fattoush (page 152). I prefer it added late or to serve: a sprinkle on raita, hummus or on rice; over fish, fried or roasted chicken or flatbreads.

Pictured opposite.

TAMARIND

Affinities

Aubergine (eggplant)
Cabbage
Cauliflower
Chicken
Coconut
Dairy
Fish
Fruit
Grains
Lamb
Lentils
Mushrooms
Pork
Potato
Rice
Root vegetables
Shellfish

Tamarind is the seedy pulp extricated from the long bean-like pods of the tropical, evergreen tamarind tree, native of Madagascar. It has little scent but a wonderful mix of acidic, sweet and fruitiness to its flavour – perfectly described by Niki Segnit in *The Flavour Thesaurus* as 'a date that sucked a lemon' – that makes it essential for spicy condiments such as Worcestershire sauce and brown sauce (page 95).

Using

Tamarind is used to sour curries, sauces, stews and soups in India and much of South East Asia, and to flavour drinks, pickles and other preserves and marinades. I find it works especially well in bringing its fruity sourness to fish curries. Tamarind is available in a few forms, from dried block to pulp to paste: the block (often including the seeds) that is reconstituted with water is where I find the most intense, fullest flavour comes, but when time is against you and convenience your friend, pulp and pastes can work brilliantly as well. Tamarind chutney should be in everyone's arsenal: heat 200g (7oz) tamarind paste, 200g (7oz) sugar, a teaspoon each of ground cumin and salt, and half a teaspoon each of chilli powder, ground pepper and ground ginger until gently simmering; allow to cool before serving.

TONKA BEANS

Affinities

Apple

Chicken

Dairy

Eggs

Fish

Rhubarb

Rice

Seafood

Tomato

This is such a peculiar spice. The beans are the weird wrinkled seeds of the huge South America cumaru tree, that are dried slowly over months – they may get a soaking in rum part way through the process – until firm and easy to grate. The flavour is quite something: an unusual but exquisite coming together of vanilla, clove, coconut, cherry and liquorice. Tonka beans are toxic in large quantities – so are tomatoes – and while banned in some countries, they are widely used, especially in France.

Using

A little tonka bean goes a long way. I think the flavour works best when not overwhelmed by large characters: in ice cream (page 231), custards and even grated over gently flavoured savoury dishes such as scallops and soufflés. Tonka beans infuse in spirits really beautifully: add a little to the ratafia on page 254.

Pictured opposite.

TURMERIC

Blends

Bumbu paste

Cape Malay spice blend

Garam masala

Hawaij

Niter kibbeh

Ras el hanout

Affinities

Aubergine (eggplant)

Beans

Cauliflower

Dairy

Eggs

Fish

Lamb

Lentils

Onion

Pork

Potato

Rice

Root vegetables

Squash

Tomato

White chocolate

As much as we might know turmeric for the kitchen, it has a history at least as significant as a dye and medicine in southern Asia from whence it hails. It is related to ginger, growing in tough tuberous clumps. Fresh it is bright yet pungent in flavour, tasting of light citrus and ginger; dried it carries much of that but somehow more densely; it is earthier and more woody. It is the scaffold on which other spices stand in many curry powder blends.

Using

Fresh turmeric keeps for a few weeks in the fridge; dried ground has a good shelf life of at least a year without losing character. Dried turmeric has a flavour that while not wildly strong is very apparent – it inhabits a spot on the flavour spectrum uncrowded by others – so a little is usually enough, and it is usually best in combination, where it colours the space between other spices, enhancing them and drawing them into a coherent whole. Use turmeric in tagines, curries, stews and soups, to add pungency and colour in piccalilli (page 83). Toss cauliflower pieces through olive oil, mixed with a little turmeric, chilli and salt, and roast for 15 minutes on high for a quick, easy, special side. Use sparingly if it's the solo spice.

VANILLA

Affinities

Apple

Banana

Black beans

Blackberries

Chocolate

Citrus

Coffee

Dairy

Fish

Melon

Pastry and cakes

Pear

Pineapple

Rhubarb

Seafood

Stone fruit

Strawberries

Sugar

Sweet potato

Tomato

Walnuts

Of the many facts you discover when writing a food book of this sort, perhaps the most startling to me is that vanilla pods – the fruit of a few species of orchid – have no scent or flavour until fermentation develops that wonderfully perfumed, sweet, warm prunes, rich vanilla character we know so well. I had trouble thinking of it as a spice in some ways as it has no edge, however gentle, to its flavour or scent: it is a feet-in-a-cool-pool-on-a-summer's-day pleasure.

Using

As a child brought up on vanilla essence, moving on to extract, and finally the long slender liquorice lace-like pods, may I counsel you to never use the first, to have a bottle of the extract on call for brownies and the like, and to use a good supplier for the pods: quality makes all the difference to the wholeness of the flavour and scent. Look for plump, dark-coloured pods. Pods are usually sliced lengthways, with the numerous tiny seeds released with the point of a knife; the pod may or may not be used in the recipe too; if not, the pod can be stored in a jar of caster sugar or vodka for its flavour to infuse. Vanilla's affinity for all things dairy sees it widely employed in cakes, puddings, creams, trifles and other desserts; used sparingly it can work surprisingly well with crustacea, fish and tomatoes too. When using good-quality vanilla, expect some variation in flavour with origin: Indonesian is often stronger than Madagascan, Mexican (the region of its origin) tends to be fruitiest, and so on. Keep stored in an airtight container out of the light.

VERBENA BERRIES

Blends

Mulled spice

Affinities

Cake and biscuits

Carrots

Chicken

Courgette (zucchini)

Duck

Fish

Pear

Rhubarb

Stone fruit

Strawberries

As the official spokesman on behalf of the Lemon Verbena Party, this may be the spice I've most enjoyed using in the last few years that is new to me. Dried verbena berries have that wonderful, clean sherbet lemon flavour carried by lemon verbena leaves, to which it is unrelated in any way but flavour.

Using

The berries – whole or ground – bring bright lemon to fish, chicken, fruit and vegetables, without any souring effect. Either allow the berries to infuse before removing them, or reduce them to a dust to sprinkle over fruit, creamy desserts or cocktails.

WATTLESEED

Affinities

Beef

Biscuit

Chicken

Chocolate

Coffee

Dairy

Eggs

Fish

Lamb

Mushrooms

Nuts

Pastry and cakes

Sweet potato

Wattleseed is the seed of a few of the edible species of acacia that grow in Australia, where it has a long history of culinary use by indigenous people. The seeds are roasted and ground into a deliciously nutty, chocolatey, raisiny, coffee-ish powder that sits especially happily with all those flavours when used.

Using

Wattleseed releases its flavour readily into water and fats; try it as an alternative to the pepper in the long pepper cream on page 226, in a cheesecake base or filling, in meringues, to flavour a crust for fish or lamb, and in the shortbread on page 217. Don't cook it for long, as it can become bitter. Traditionally used in damper – a loaf cooked in the embers of a fire – it adds a wonderful nuttiness and depth to soda bread; a couple of tablespoons is ideal.

THE SPICE BLENDS

While there is considerable celebration in these pages of the solo spice, there is equally so of the happy comings together, the holy alliances and the perfect pairings that can bring such pleasure: these blends are yours to play with. There are master recipes for classic spice mixes, such as garam masala, Chinese five-spice, chaat masala and hawaij; they are all excellent as they are, but I hope that with confidence you'll start to adapt them to suit your palate and the recipe. Make the garam masala earthier with more cumin and less star anise, add more fire to the gunpowder mix with hotter chillies or the reverse, as you wish.

As much as most blends have a rich history of use and classic recipes to which they are put, don't be afraid to play. The tempero baiano cabbage on page 129 is as far from an 'authentic' pairing as a Chinese five-spice Eton mess would be, but it is no less delicious for it. Try the cabbage with any of the spice blends that take your fancy, and carry on from there. I especially recommend using spice blends to finish soups, dusted over roasted vegetables to serve; eggs – fried or poached – on toast seem happy to accommodate and show off virtually any spice blend to fine effect.

Make these blends in smallish amounts, as they will lose essential character to varying degrees from the moment they are ground and combined. Keep small jars for storing them handy, use masking tape to label them (no more sticky, half washed up, stubborn label remnants under the thumbnail for you) and keep jarred blends out of direct sunlight.

Unless otherwise advised or where no method is given:

- before using/grinding, lightly toast whole seed spices in a dry pan over a low–medium heat, agitating the pan to prevent them burning.

- reduce the spices to a powder before using.

- don't dry-toast ground spices. Only once will you want to choke on cayenne that has taken flight from a hot dry pan and reconvened at the back of your throat and under your eyelids.

ADVIEH

An aromatic, sweet spice blend from Persia (now Iran) that sits happily in sweet or savoury dishes. It takes particularly well to lentils, stews, used as a rub for meat and sprinkled over creamy desserts, but you may find that – as with chaat – you keep some handy to use more widely, as in its native country. Advieh is hugely variable around a core recipe, so do tweak to suit whatever it will accompany: a little coriander, dried lime, pepper or clove is not uncommon, especially when used in cooking rather than added to serve.

4 tbsp dried rose petals

1 tbsp ground cardamom seeds

2 tbsp ground cumin

2 tbsp ground cinnamon

1 tbsp ground ginger

BERBERE

An Ethiopian blend that carries as much kick as it does intense aroma. It is classically used in stews – especially the wonderful wats of Ethiopia (page 182) – but it makes an equally good rub for meat ahead of cooking. A tweak of ajowan is not uncommonly included. I like dark, earthy Mexican Cascabel chillies for this, but the choice is yours.

2 tsp coriander seeds

1 tsp cumin seeds

1 tsp fenugreek seeds

1 tsp black peppercorns, ideally long pepper

4 allspice berries

6 green cardamom pods, seeds only

6 cloves

1 medium-hot dried chilli

2 tbsp sweet paprika

1 tsp salt

½ nutmeg

½ tsp ground ginger

½ tsp ground cinnamon

BAHARAT

Originating from Turkey and its neighbours, baharat is delightful mix of the warm, aromatic, earthy, floral and the fiery; it is bold without being insistent. The name covers a multitude of variations: find yourself in Istanbul and the baharat might contain dried mint, in Tunis it might be heavier with cinnamon, and so on. This version is perhaps more Iraqi in composition, and nicely fragrant. As well as making a dry rub prior to cooking or marinade, baharat is so good as an all-purpose seasoning; try it dusted on sweet potato wedges (page 134) or the spiced sweetcorn (page 127)

2 tbsp cumin seeds

2 tbsp black peppercorns

1 tbsp coriander seeds

2 allspice berries

6 cloves

5cm (2in) cassia, or cinnamon stick

6 green cardamom pods, seeds only (optional)

1 crushed dried lime (optional)

2 tbsp unsmoked paprika

a really generous scratching of nutmeg

Add all but the paprika and nutmeg to a pan and toast over a low heat until the scent rises. Whizz to a powder in a spice grinder or mortar and pestle, then add the paprika and nutmeg.

BLACKENING SEASONING

A classic Cajun blend that's used widely across the Deep South of the USA and is central to blackening recipes (page 172) where meat or fish are coated in this and cooked at high temperatures. There's not a whole load that's subtle about this blend: all its lights are on full beam to stand up to the frying. The choice of paprika is entirely yours.

2 tsp paprika or smoked paprika

1 tsp chilli powder

1 tsp salt

1 tsp garlic powder

1 tsp dried oregano

1 tsp dried thyme

½ tsp onion powder

½ tsp freshly ground black pepper

½ tsp cayenne, or to taste

CAPE MALAY SPICE BLEND

This originates from the community of Muslims concentrated largely in Cape Town, on South Africa's west coast, whose descendants – of their own accord and otherwise – came to live and work in the country under Dutch and British rule during the 17–19th centuries. It is a wonderful blend, beautifully balanced between fragrant, earthy and sweet and commonly used as a marinade, meat rub, in curries and stews. While gentle as a default, you can up the heat with the chilli if you prefer.

1 tbsp coriander seeds

1 tbsp cumin seeds

1 tsp black mustard seeds

1 tsp fennel seeds

2 tsp fenugreek seeds

1 tsp black peppercorns

1 tbsp cardamom seeds

4 cloves

10 dried curry leaves

1 tsp ground turmeric

1 tsp ground ginger

1 tbsp cayenne, or to taste

BUMBU PASTE

Bumbu is an umbrella for endless variations on this classic spice paste from across the kitchens of the thousands of Indonesian islands. It provides the heart of excellent sauces and marinades for meat, fish and poultry. Candlenuts are the classic nut here, and while they can be sourced online, they are mildly toxic raw and need thorough cooking: the more widely available (and perfectly safe) macadamia nuts work equally well. Long pepper is ideal; black peppercorns will do. A makrut lime leaf and/or the seeds from a couple of cardamom pods can be added if you fancy. This freezes well, so make plenty if you prefer.

2 cloves

3 tsp coriander seeds

1 tsp black peppercorns

¼ tsp white peppercorns

¼ tsp cumin seeds

1 tsp sesame seeds

3 macadamia nuts

¼ tsp freshly grated nutmeg

2 tbsp grated galangal

2cm (¾in) fresh turmeric, finely chopped (or replace with 2 tsp ground turmeric)

1 tbsp grated fresh ginger

3 shallots, finely chopped

3 garlic cloves, finely chopped

2 bird's-eye chillies, finely chopped

¼ tsp shrimp paste (optional)

1 bay leaf

1 lemongrass stalk, finely chopped

2 tbsp coconut oil or sunflower oil

good pinch of salt

In a dry frying pan over a moderate heat, lightly toast the whole spices and sesame seeds. Grind with the nuts in a pestle and mortar or electric grinder. Add the nutmeg. Add the rest of the ingredients and blend the paste with a stick blender or similar.

CHAAT MASALA

This Indian spice blend is an extraordinary coming together of sweet, sour, pungent and earthy that brings intensity, depth and brightness to curries, dhals, salads and so much more. Try it on roasted vegetables – before and after cooking.

2 tbsp cumin seeds

1 tbsp fennel seeds

1 tbsp coriander seeds

1½ tbsp ajowan seeds

2 whole cloves or ½ tsp ground cloves

½ tsp asafoetida

1 tbsp amchoor

1 tbsp sea salt

1 tbsp Kashmiri dried chilli powder

¼ tsp ground ginger

1 tbsp dried mint (optional)

CHINESE FIVE-SPICE

Perhaps the most widely known of China's regional cuisines, the sweet-sour, aromatic cooking of Guangdong in the south is home to the famous five-spice. Widely available in shops as it may be, this spice blend has a lively intensity when homemade that is so very different. Try it in stir fries, stews, as a dry rub for meat, with squash, seafood, mixed with honey and soy as a marinade, and with stone fruit, especially plums.

2 whole star anise

2 tsp fennel seeds

10cm (4in) cassia or cinnamon stick

2 tsp Sichuan peppercorns

8 cloves

CHIMICHURRI

This Andean sauce is a fiery coming together of spice and herbs that suits the kind of hard cooking that comes with flames and smoke. Chimichurri is fantastic with meat, roasted vegetables, fish and roast potatoes, where its big flavours and oily acidity shine.

4 tbsp red wine vinegar

½ tsp salt

2 garlic cloves, finely chopped

1 small shallot, finely chopped (or use ½ bunch of trimmed spring onions/scallions)

½ tsp chilli flakes, or more to taste

1 tsp good-quality dried oregano

small bunch of parsley, finely chopped

2 tbsp fresh oregano (optional)

6 tbsp extra virgin olive oil (or vegetable oil)

sea salt and freshly ground black pepper

Mix together the vinegar, salt, garlic and shallot and put to one side for 10 minutes. Stir in the rest of the ingredients and allow the flavours to get to know each other for an hour or so before serving.

CINNAMON SUGAR

Every now and then, Sunday breakfast needs a sweet nudge: this is the golden ticket. Dust heavily over generously buttered toast and flash under the grill (broiler) before serving, or sprinkle over eggy bread as it leaves the pan, its oil catching the spicy sweetness. I appreciate this might sound risky but bear with me – dust a little over almost-cooked bacon, for it to work its magic in the last minute of cooking.

4cm (1½in) cinnamon stick

4 tbsp caster (superfine) sugar

Whizz together in an electric grinder until reduced to a powder.

CUMIN SALT

As with cinnamon sugar, a recipe that's really clinging by its fingertips to what can call itself a recipe. It is here because it is impossible not to share its simple brilliance with you. On chips, fried eggs, panisse (page 112), a peculiarly splendid variation on michelada (page 256) and on pretty much any flatbread. I could go on. A pinch of paprika or chilli flakes (chipotle, especially) is a great variation.

2 tbsp cumin seeds

3 tbsp salt

Combine the seeds with the salt and whizz in a spice grinder (or use a mortar and pestle) to reduce the seeds to a coarse powder.

SWEET DUKKAH

This gorgeous variation brings crunch where softness might otherwise dominate: poached pears and yoghurt become something very different with a generous dash of this. This is my favourite combination that you can adapt as you like – a knuckle of star anise or an inch of cinnamon, hazelnuts instead of pistachios, use the sweeter, nuttier black sesame if you have only them, and so on. The coriander is not ground; being reduced only to coarse pieces brings its flavour in distinct punctuation rather than as part of the whole.

2 blades of mace

2 cloves

2 cinnamon berries

2 Ethiopian passion berries

100g (3½oz) pistachios

2 tbsp coriander seeds

2 tbsp white sesame seeds

Toast the mace, cloves, cinnamon berries and passion berries until they start to release their scent. Use a pestle and mortar or spice grinder to reduce them to a fairly fine powder. Toast the nuts, coriander and sesame in the dry pan until the nuts and sesame seeds start to brown just a touch. Add them to the spices and whizz/pound until the nuts have become a coarse rubble.

DUKKAH

With the Red and Mediterranean seas lapping it its shores, Egypt wasn't short of spice trade. Dukkah is a pretty good shorthand of what resulted: a fresh, nutty, earthy coming together of nuts, spices and sesame seeds. Cumin is a characteristic ingredient of so many Egyptian recipes and here its earthy nuttiness ties the pistachios to the spices beautifully. There are many variations in ingredients and quantities but after a long time of adding more ingredients or differing quantities, this simple version makes me happiest. Adding a teaspoon of nigella seeds makes a fine variation. Serve with excellent oil and bread, and scatter on soups and wherever its special character might suit.

100g (3½oz) shelled pistachios (or use blanched almonds)

2 tbsp coriander seeds

2 tbsp cumin seeds

3 tbsp sesame seeds (black or white)

pinch of fennel seeds

sea salt and freshly ground black pepper

Dry-fry all the seeds and nuts in a frying pan for 2–3 minutes until just fragrant. Use a pestle and mortar or food processor (or a sturdy bowl and a rolling pin handle) to grind very coarsely, then season to taste with salt and pepper.

DURBAN CURRY POWDER

Perhaps as much as any country, South Africa has experienced a wide range of culinary influences to go with those indigenous, due to exploration and colonialism courtesy of the Dutch, Portuguese and British among others. Durban's position on the eastern coast with the Indian Ocean lapping at its toes was prime for widespread trade, and it has long enjoyed a large Indian population. Durban loves a curry, and this distinctive sweet/hot blend shows off its Indian influences perfectly.

2 tbsp coriander seeds
2 tbsp cumin seeds
12 cardamom pods, seeds only
2 tsp fenugreek seeds
8cm (3in) cinnamon stick
2 cloves
1 ½ tsp ground ginger
2 tbsp mild chilli powder
1 tbsp cayenne

SWEET GARAM MASALA

This sweet blend is anchored beautifully by the black pepper, keeping its feet firmly away from any hint of cloying. This is so good on rice pudding, poached fruit, fresh or roasted figs, and even on carrots and other vegetables prior to roasting. A little star anise and/or fennel seed is great in this too if it suits what it will be accompanying.

40 green cardamom pods, seeds only
10cm (4in) cinnamon stick
2 generous blades of mace
16 cloves
2 tsp black peppercorns

GARAM MASALA

Garam masala means hot spices, which is not to imply chilli heat: cloves, black pepper, cinnamon and black cardamom are spices that create heat in the body. Characteristic of northern Indian cooking originally, it has spread considerably: there are more versions of garam masala than there are awful, post-pub-gathering strangulations of 'Summertime' by someone too indebted to the apple or the hop, which is saying something. Here I present mine, or more accurately Sumayya Usmani's and mine, which are differently excellent. Sumayya's recipe is a sweeter version of my own core recipe: the quantity of green cardamom being the main difference. Although I often add garam masala early when cooking to add welcome earthiness, I almost always use it late too, for a brighter dose of the flavours and aromas.

2 large black cardamom pods, seeds only
1 cinnamon stick
1 lantern of mace
10 cloves
10 black peppercorns
2 tsp black cumin seeds
1 tbsp coriander seeds
1 tbsp anise seed
10–12 green cardamom pods, seeds only
2 whole star anise

GUNPOWDER MIX

Gunpowder (aka milaga/milagai podi) is from southern India, and typifies the bold bright flavours of that region. As you might imagine, its name refers to the heat – traditionally imparted by Kashmiri chillies – that drives this blend along. There are endless versions, varying with region and individual taste: I love the balance of heat, sour, pungent and aromatic here, but do feel free to embellish as you wish. It is so beautifully versatile: try it sprinkled over dosas, stir into rice with a little oil, and in the gunpowder potatoes on page 132.

2 tsp coriander seeds	
1 tbsp poppy seeds	
2 tsp toasted cumin seeds	
1 tsp black peppercorns	
1 tsp fenugreek seeds	
1 ½ tsp sesame seeds	
1 tbsp red lentils	
1–2 medium-hot dried chillies	
½ tsp salt	
1 ½ tbsp amchoor	

HAWAIJ

A somewhat curry powder-like blend from Israel and Yemen that is one of my favourites sprinkled on pretty much anything savoury. As with garam masala, there are sweeter versions: anise, ginger and fennel are the usual additions.

4 tbsp black peppercorns	
5 tbsp cumin seeds	
6 cardamom pods, seeds only	
1 tbsp ground coriander	
3 cloves	
2 tbsp ground turmeric	
pinch of salt	

HARISSA

The Maghreb – where Europe meets Africa meets the Middle East – has such a wealth of earthy, sweet, rich recipes, with plenty of intense exuberant flavours. Harissa is one such: every ingredient is present and alive on the tongue. I make this relatively loose, but ease back on the oil if you prefer. As inauthentic as it may be, I like the level of heat and flavour of the chillies below, which reflects the more common medium mildness of most harissas: if you favour the more intense heat of Tunisian harissa, choose chillies – dried or fresh – to suit.

2 large dried New Mexico chillies	
2 tbsp coriander seeds	
2 tbsp caraway seeds	
2 tbsp cumin seeds	
3 tbsp guajillo chilli flakes	
6 fat garlic cloves	
1 tsp salt	
100ml (3 ½ fl oz) olive oil, plus a little extra	
juice of 1 lemon	

Pour boiling water over the dried chillies and allow to rehydrate for 30 minutes. Drain the chillies, slice them lengthways, removing and discarding the stalks and seeds. Pour away the water. Grind the spice seeds to a medium coarse powder. In a food processor – I find a hand blender best for this sort of amount – whizz together all the ingredients until a fairly smoothish paste results. Transfer to a jar and drizzle a little oil on the surface to seal it. In theory this will last for a month or two in the fridge, but in practice you'll be out of it by the weekend.

JERK SEASONING

When European explorers reached the islands of the Caribbean, they set about an aggressive colonization. The area became a crucial focus for spice trading, and much of its bold, contrasting, upfront cuisine reflects those influences. Jerk seasoning – originating in Jamaica and adopted and adapted widely since – is a Caribbean classic, as is the jerk chicken (page 178) that shows it off so well. As you'd imagine, variations around the theme are many: some add onion and/or garlic powder, the thyme might be dried, there might be cloves, paprika or perhaps a pinch or two of sugar, and so on. This is how I like it; I hope you do too.

1 tsp salt

2 tsp ground allspice

½ tsp grated nutmeg

1 tsp ground ginger, or 1 tbsp grated fresh ginger

1 tsp ground black pepper

½ tsp ground cinnamon

1 tbsp fresh thyme leaves

1–2 tsp chilli flakes

LEBKUCHENGEWÜRZ

One sniff of this German gingerbread spice mix and I am ready for winter. It is the definition of festive. Whether you are making gingerbread or the lebkuchen biscuits on page 216, this is what you need. A good pinch over rice pudding and other desserts is almost always rewarded. And hot chocolate. This is slightly on the cardamom side, which is just how I like life. It's not 100 miles away from the Finnish gingerbread spice, or indeed many other gingery spice blends for biscuits around the world.

6cm (2½in) cinnamon stick

10 cloves

10 allspice berries

1 lantern of mace

10 cardamom pods, seeds only

½ tsp ground ginger

1 tsp anise seed

KHMELI-SUNELI

This Georgian festival of dried herbs and spices is quite the coming-together of warm, aromatic, cool and biting. There is much variation: dried tarragon, dried hyssop and dried parsley often feature; garlic powder is common; fenugreek leaves are often used instead, as well as the seeds. Dried marigold is available online (see page 266); it brings colour and freshness. Blue fenugreek is a milder, less bitter version of the more widely available kind; if you don't have the former, substitute with a little less of the latter. Use this as a general, all-purpose seasoning; I'd suggest it's best added late, dusted on roasted vegetables, on soups and stews to serve.

1 tbsp blue fenugreek seeds

1 tbsp coriander seeds

1 tsp black peppercorns

3 bay leaves, each torn into 3 or 4 pieces

1 tsp chilli powder, or more to taste

1 tbsp dill seed

2 tbsp dried marjoram

2 tbsp dried marigold

1 tbsp dried mint

4 tsp salt

MIXED SPICE

Ah, the much-maligned mixed spice, victim of so many ill-judged blendings of inferior spices. I hope you'll let this put the matter to rights. Apples, pork, plums, figs, peaches and pastry are a few of the many places to be using mixed spice. The cardamom and coriander are options I favour more than not. For a slightly sweeter mix, replace the nutmeg with 2 teaspoons of ground mace.

6cm (2½in) cinnamon stick

4 cloves

1 tsp coriander seeds (optional)

5 cardamom pods, seeds only (optional)

½ nutmeg

1 tsp ground allspice

1 tsp ground ginger

MULLING SPICES

Sometimes a cigar of cinnamon, a couple of cloves and an asterisk of star anise is all you need when mulling cider, wine or apple juice, but if you are looking for something a little more complex, this is for you: tweak it to suit the cider, juice or wine and to your taste.

2 cloves

3 whole star anise

6 allspice berries

6 Ethiopian passion berries

6 cinnamon berries

6 verbena berries

6 green cardamom pods, seeds only

PANCH PHORAN

Just in front of the mixer, to the left of the best vinegar and to the right of the bottle of olive oil sits a little jar of panch phoran. I've never not got some of this Bengali/Bangladeshi blend on the go to sprinkle on soups, finish lentil dishes or even dash over poached eggs. 'Panch' translates as five and 'phoran' as spice, and the quantities extend this simplicity: equal parts of five complementing spices, that stay whole – simply mix the seeds together. I use it as often raw as a condiment, fried in ghee or oil as it is most commonly deployed.

1 tbsp cumin seeds

1 tbsp fennel seeds

1 tbsp nigella seeds

1 tbsp fenugreek seeds

1 tbsp mustard seeds

NITER KIBBEH

This Ethiopian spiced clarified butter is the most extraordinary thing; a hymn to the power of spices working together to a greater whole. And it almost makes itself. One taste, and I suspect you will find no shortage of uses to which you want to put it (see introduction, page 13). Start by slathering it on a crumpet, and then make the doro wat (page 182) and you'll be away. I used Mexican oregano for its citrus zing, but straight dried oregano is equally if differently good here. Although it will keep on the side for a week or two, keep it in the fridge where it will be good for a couple of months at least.

Makes about 450ml (1 pint)

1 tsp black peppercorns

4 black cardamom pods, torn open

4 cloves

2 tsp fenugreek seeds

1 tbsp coriander seeds

1 tbsp cumin seeds

1 lantern of mace

500g (1lb 2oz) unsalted butter, cut into cubes

2 large garlic cloves, sliced

5cm (2in) fresh ginger, peeled and sliced

6cm (2½in) cinnamon stick

1 tbsp dried oregano

good pinch of ground turmeric

Add all the spices (except the cinnamon) to a medium pan and toast over a low heat. Add the butter and the remaining ingredients and bring slowly to a bare simmer. Allow to bubble very gently for an hour, during which time the fats will separate out and the flavours infuse. Pour through a fine muslin into a jug, catching the spices and fatty foam. Decant into a jar and allow to cool.

QALAT DAQQA

This Tunisian five-spice makes me happy.
It embellishes savoury and sweet with equal
enthusiasm, though even if I could only smell
rather than taste it I'd keep a jar on the side.
Classically, it brings sweet warmth to marinades
and when dusted on vegetables, tagines and other
stews, but is one to use generously wherever you
get the urge. The cake on page 223 is a fine
example of its versatility.

2 tsp black peppercorns

1 tbsp grains of paradise

1 whole nutmeg, bashed and grated, or 2 tbsp grated

14 cloves

6cm (2½in) cinnamon stick

QUATRE ÉPICES

France may not seem like a hive of spiced recipes,
but there is more than might be initially obvious.
The ports brought considerable spice trading and
local recipes sprang up reflecting this – mouclade
(page 164) for one. Cloves and nutmeg became
popular ingredients in French cuisine in the 1700s,
and this wonderful blend owes much to those days.
Quatre épices is famously used to spice terrines
and patés; occasionally, you might find a fifth
interloper in the form of cinnamon.

2 tbsp ground white pepper

1 tbsp ground ginger

1 tbsp grated nutmeg

1 tbsp ground cloves

RAS EL HANOUT

If there's one spice blend for which there are more
versions than McCartney's 'Yesterday', it's ras el
hanout. Its literal translation as 'top of the shop'
implies the best of what's available, and that might
be at least partly why it is so varied by country,
region and kitchen. This flexibility allows you to
tweak it to suit the savoury or sweet, and makes it
as at home with monkfish and lamb as it is in
pastilla (page 203) or in Nargisse's banana bread
(page 224).

I'm including the spices in ground form here to
show the relative proportions more clearly.

1 tsp ground cassia or cinnamon

1 tsp ground allspice

1 tsp fennel or anise seed

1 tsp ground cumin

1 tsp ground mace

1 tsp ground coriander

1 tsp cayenne

1 tsp ground ginger

½ tsp ground green cardamom seeds

½ tsp ground long pepper

½ tsp ground cubeb pepper

½ tsp ground grains of paradise

pinch of ground cloves

Optional extras

a few strands of saffron

1 whole black cardamom, ground

½ tsp paprika

½ tsp ground turmeric

1 tsp dried rose petals

½ tsp dried lavender flowers

½ tsp caraway

1 bay leaf, ground

SAJJI MASALA

This spice blend, courtesy of Sumayya Usmani, has a wonderful balance between earthy, sweet, sour and aromatic, and in contrast with some sajji masalas, its bite is solely from the pepper – by all means add chilli if the recipe would benefit. Try this with the chicken sajji (page 188) and you may find – as I did – that other ideas for using it will fall into your mind: dusted over a whole cauliflower for one.

2 tbsp cumin seeds	
2 tbsp whole black peppercorns	
6 green cardamom pods, seeds only	
3 tbsp coriander seeds	
1 tbsp fennel seeds	
½ tsp kalanamak (black salt), or sea salt	
1 tbsp amchoor	

SOUR CHILLI SEASONING

Tajín is a widely available Mexican brand of seasoning, made with mild dried chillies, salt and dried lime juice. It is quite something. This takes its spirit, replacing the dehydrated lime juice with dried limes. The nature of the chilli is yours to choose: I like a deeply flavoured but only gently hot chilli, such as New Mexico or ancho: if I'm in the mood for heat I can always over-the-top it with another livelier chilli powder; perhaps some cayenne. This works really well with amchoor instead of the black lime too.

1 tsp sea salt	
2 black limes, lightly crushed	
1 New Mexico chilli	

SHICHIMI TOGARASHI

This is Yuki Gomi's version of the classic Japanese seven-spice. Aonori is available online and in some shops. Try it in the ramen on page 158 or on grilled meat; it is superb used as a livener like pepper, on chips especially. The skin from one satsuma should make around 2–3 teaspoons of dried powder.

Makes 20g (¾ oz)

2 tsp dried satsuma skin or yuzu peel powder	
2 tsp ichimi togarashi or dried red chilli	
1 tsp hemp seeds	
1 tsp black sesame seeds	
1 tsp roasted white sesame seeds	
1 tsp aonori	
½ tsp Sansho pepper	

Dry the satsuma peel in the oven for 30–40 minutes at 95°C/200°F/gas mark ¼, then grind it into a fine powder. Grind the hemp seeds and the dried chilli into a powder. Mix everything together.

SRI LANKAN CURRY POWDER

This blend is beautifully warm and aromatic, featuring cinnamon and cardamom – both native to the island – at its heart. Sri Lankan curries often feature coconut milk, fish and seafood, which this spice mix complements so well. The basmati rice adds a wonderful nutty, buttery, roasted flavour: lightly toast with the whole seed spices before grinding everything together. There is only heat from the peppercorns here: add 1 dried chilli (strength of your choosing) to the blend, or, as I prefer, just use fresh chilli when making the curry.

2 tbsp coriander seeds	
1 tbsp cumin seeds	
8cm (3in) cinnamon stick	
12 cardamom pods, seeds only	
3 cloves	
2 tsp black peppercorns	
20 curry leaves	
1 tbsp uncooked basmati rice	

SVANURI MARILI

Also known as Svaneti salt, after the mountainous region of Georgia, in Europe, from whence it hails. This is such a fine mix of flavours, though it keeps for only a day or two as the garlic declines and takes the rest with it. Use it in dressings, to season, or on the Svaneti potatoes on page 133.

1 tbsp coriander seeds

1 tbsp blue fenugreek seeds

2 tsp chilli powder

1 tsp dill seeds (optional)

4 garlic cloves, finely chopped

3 tbsp salt

TIMUR KO CHOP

A lively salt and pepper seasoning embellished with chilli powder of a strength to suit, with variations throughout the Himalayas and Sichuan regions. Garlic often features. Sprinkle wherever your fancy takes.

1 tsp Sichuan peppercorns

1 tsp chilli powder

1 tsp salt

TEMPERO BAIANO

A big bold blend from the Bahia region on Brazil's east coast. Classically used to season meat and fish recipes, but really special added to soups and vegetable dishes to serve. I prefer unsmoked paprika but the choice is yours; black pepper in place of white is good too.

1 tbsp coriander seeds

2 tsp cumin seeds

1 tsp white peppercorns

1 tsp cayenne

1 tbsp paprika

½ tsp onion powder

½ tsp garlic powder

5 tsp dried oregano

Lightly toast the coriander, cumin and peppercorns, then reduce to a coarse powder in a spice blender and mix with the rest of the ingredients.

YANGNYEOMJANG

This is such a great Korean sauce that doubles very well as a dip or marinade. That said, the place to try it first is probably with the fried fish on page 172. If you don't have gochugaru – Korean chilli flakes – you can substitute with either fresh or another dried chilli. A little rice vinegar can sometimes be good here, to straighten it out with a little acidity: half a teaspoon at best.

60ml (4 tbsp) soy sauce

½ bunch of spring onions (scallions), thinly sliced

2 garlic cloves, finely chopped

1 green chilli, finely chopped

1 tbsp gochugaru flakes

2 tsp sugar

4 tsp sesame oil

1 tbsp toasted sesame seeds

Combine all the ingredients in a bowl and stir to thoroughly combine.

ZHUG

Zhug commonly features in Israeli recipes, but Yemen is its spiritual home. Fiery, aromatic and herby, this 'goes with everything'. Try it with sausages, potatoes, roast vegetables and more.

4 cardamom pods, seeds only

1 tsp black peppercorns

1 tsp coriander seeds

1 tsp cumin seeds

4 serrano chillies, finely chopped

2 garlic cloves, chopped

small bunch of parsley, finely chopped

small bunch of coriander (cilantro), finely chopped

60ml (4 tbsp) olive oil

juice of ½ lemon

sea salt

Toast the spices in a dry pan over a low–medium heat, then grind. Blend everything together: I use a stick blender and keep the consistency rough.

ZA'ATAR

This Middle Eastern blend – Syrian in origin but since widespread – is one you may well find yourself sprinkling on everything from oily flatbreads to labneh to eggs on toast to mixed salads to smashed cucumbers to chickpea soups. It makes a great dry seasoning for meat and fish prior to cooking, as well as when scattered over pretty much anything to finish.

3 tbsp sesame seeds

1 ½ tbsp ground cumin

2 tbsp ground sumac

2 tbsp dried Mexican oregano, or dried marjoram, oregano, savory, or hyssop

1 tbsp salt

Lightly toast the sesame seeds in a pan over a medium heat, shuffling them around a bit to ensure they don't turn too dark. Combine all the ingredients together in a mortar and pestle, as much as anything to encourage the flavours and scents to be released as they mix.

SMALL THINGS

SPICED APPLES AND PEARS

Every autumn I make a handful of recipes that mark the season. Medlar sticky toffee pudding, sloe gin in quantities I rarely get through, quince vodka, and this, a classic sweet/sour recipe where the spices really sing. One year I might go heavy with star anise, another it might be cloves that lead: this autumn, this remarkable spice combination. I hope you like it. If you are making two batches, cinnamon berries in place of the passion berries is really worth trying.

Fills a 1 litre (2 pint) jar

500g (1lb 2oz) caster (superfine) sugar

250ml (9fl oz) white wine vinegar

250ml (9fl oz) cider vinegar

zest of 1 lemon

10cm (4in) fresh ginger, thinly sliced

2 bay leaves

1 tsp black peppercorns

1 tsp Ethiopian passion berries

1 tsp juniper berries

8 small, squat, firm pears

4 firm apples

Put all but the fruit in a large non-reactive pan and bring to a simmer, stirring to dissolve the sugar. Leave over a low heat.

Peel the pears and apples and add them to the simmering liquid as you go. Cook until almost tender: 20 minutes should do, but test with the point of a knife.

Use a spoon to lower the fruit into the jar. Pour the liquid over the fruit – there may be the smallest amount left over; this varies with shape of jar – and seal the jar immediately. Allow to infuse for a few days before trying. They will last at least until the daffs start to appear in the shops in spring.

BREAD AND BUTTER PICKLES

A classic pickle from the Great Depression years in the USA, when this was a cheap and delicious way of brightening up a bread and butter sandwich. A cheese or ham roll is immeasurably improved by its presence, and I have to say – true to its heritage – just this pickle in a buttered roll, unaccompanied, is mighty fine. Two things: be accurate with the turmeric or it will dominate, and don't overcook, as the spices are simmered for just long enough to activate and release their flavour without blurring into each other. This is one of those times when using very good coriander seeds is apparent in the results.

Fills 2 x 700ml (1½ pint) jars

4–5 cucumbers (about 900g/2lb), cut into 5mm (¼in) slices

2 medium/large onions, halved and cut into 5mm (¼in) slices

60g (2¼oz) salt

320ml (11fl oz) cider vinegar

100g (3½oz) soft light brown sugar

100g (3½oz) caster (superfine) sugar

½ tsp ground turmeric

5 cloves

1½ tsp black mustard seeds

1 tsp coriander seeds

½ tsp celery seeds

Place the cucumber and onion slices in a large bowl and scatter with the salt, turning everything over with your hands to distribute it thoroughly. Place another bowl on top, add a bag of sugar or something similarly heavy and leave for 90 minutes for the vegetables beneath to release their water. Rinse the vegetables in a colander, then pat dryish using a clean tea towel.

Place the other ingredients in a pan and bring to a simmer over a medium heat, stirring to dissolve the sugar. Allow to simmer for 2–3 minutes while you place the vegetables in a large sterilized jar or two smaller ones. Remove the spiced vinegar from the heat and allow to cool for a couple of minutes. Pour the liquid over the vegetables and seal, using a pickle pebble or scrunched-up piece of baking parchment to keep the cucumber and onion submerged. Cool, then refrigerate.

Keeps for an age but is best in the first four weeks or so before the cucumber loses crunch.

BURMESE RAINBOW PICKLE by MiMi Aye

When I was very little, one of my favourite activities was to explore my grandma's kitchen in Mandalay – I'd pull out all the drawers and look in all the cupboards, and poke my finger into jars and nose into tins with great glee. There was a tall, mesh-fronted cabinet which remained a mystery as I could never get its doors open and, on top of this cabinet, stood an array of glass bottles full of lotions and potions, all labelled meticulously in handwritten, curlicued Burmese script. For, despite managing the incredible feat of having no fewer than three children who went into the medical profession, my paternal grandma, who I called Pwa Pwa, insisted on making all of her own home remedies to deal with her various ailments, imagined or otherwise. Two of these dusty bottles held tiny round balls made of ground turmeric bound with wild honey – Pwa Pwa's hands were often stained a deep ochre because she rolled each one herself, partly as a form of meditation. I remember her insisting that my mother take one of these honey-turmeric balls a day to cure her asthma; my mum would dutifully smile and nod her head and then quietly dispose of them while no one was looking. Cut to three decades later, and I walk into my parents' living room in Kent to find my mother (who also happens to be a doctor) methodically rolling these little pellets round in her own palms, as she watches the TV. I quirk an eyebrow and she looks up, grins sheepishly and says, 'I think your Pwa Pwa might have been right after all.'

Whatever the truth behind the health-giving properties of turmeric, it has long been an essential part of the arsenal in a Burmese kitchen, cropping up in curries and stir fries, salads and noodles. And unlike, say, the Thai, we tend to prefer the earthier kiss of the ground spice to the fresh root. Theezohn thanat is a pickle made up of a vibrant-tasting array of vegetables (the Burmese name literally means 'vegetable medley pickle' and you can honestly use whatever you like or whatever's in season), but it's the spices, especially the ground turmeric, which really make it – imparting an unmistakably bitter, rounded and rich twang to proceedings.

A cousin of the South East Asian acar, the pickle makes a welcome accompaniment for similarly spiced dishes; in Burma (aka Myanmar), it is mainly eaten alongside rice and Indian-inflected curries. However, it's also wonderful used wherever you would chutney – try it in a hearty sandwich, with cold meats or a cheeseboard, with a pork pie or as part of a ploughman's lunch, or simply use it to liven up your leftovers and give your palate a bit of a kick.

**Makes enough to fill a
1 litre (2 pint) jar**

1 large carrot, sliced into
semicircles

½ medium cauliflower
(about 250g/9oz), broken
up into 1cm (½in) florets

100g (3½oz) green beans,
trimmed and chopped into
2cm (¾in) lengths

2 mini cucumbers, sliced
into rounds

6 radishes, halved

6 garlic cloves, sliced (keep
the skin on)

1 tbsp caster (superfine)
sugar

1 tsp salt

100ml (3½fl oz) malt
vinegar

For the spiced oil

3 tbsp neutral oil

1 tbsp cumin seeds

1 tbsp yellow mustard seeds

1 tsp coriander seeds

1 tsp ground turmeric

½ tsp chilli flakes

Place the carrot, cauliflower and beans in a large heatproof bowl and pour over a kettle of boiling water; leave to blanch for 5 minutes. Drain and return to the bowl with the cucumber, radishes and garlic. Sprinkle the sugar and salt all over the vegetables and then drizzle the vinegar on top. Toss everything together thoroughly with your hands and then leave to marinate for 30 minutes. Drain away any excess liquid and then set the bowl next to your cooker.

Heat the oil in a small frying pan over a high heat. Add all of the spices, turn the heat down to medium and allow to sizzle, shaking the pan gently. As soon as the seeds start to pop and the spices become fragrant, remove the pan from the heat and, while it is still hot, drizzle the spiced oil over the marinated vegetables. As soon as it is cool enough to handle, use clean hands to toss everything together again. The pickle is ready to eat immediately or you can store in a jar or tub in the fridge for up to 3 days.

HARISSA PICCALILLI

Piccalilli will always feel like Christmas to me, as – for no obvious reason – the old man would only have it in the house over the festive season. And you wonder why I'm a troubled soul. This, I promise, is as good as piccalilli gets: a spicier tweak on the recipe in my book *Sour*, it has harissa driving the fragrant, lively bottom end along.

Fills 2 x 700ml (1 ½ pint) jars

1kg (2lb 4oz) washed vegetables, cut into pieces no larger than 2cm (¾ in) – I go for equal-ish amounts of sugar snaps, mini courgettes/zucchini (or usual size quartered lengthways and sliced), cauliflower and carrots

50g (2oz) fine salt

600ml (1 ¼ pints) cider vinegar

120g (4oz) granulated sugar

80g (3oz) honey

25g (1oz) cornflour (cornstarch)

4 tsp ground turmeric

4 tsp English mustard powder

3 tsp celery seeds

3 tsp fenugreek seeds

3 tsp yellow mustard seeds

3 tbsp harissa (page 66)

Ensure the vegetables are relatively dry. Place them in a large bowl and sprinkle with the salt. Turn the vegetables over to distribute the salt thoroughly, then cover and leave somewhere cool for 24 hours. Rinse with cold water and drain well.

Put 520ml (1 pint) of the vinegar into a pan with the sugar and honey and bring to the boil. While that is happening, stir the cornflour in a bowl to ensure it is lump-free, then add the spices and combine well. Add a little of the remaining vinegar to the bowl and stir into the spicy flour to create a paste. Gradually add the remaining vinegar to thin the paste a little.

Once the pan of sweetened vinegar has reached the boil, reduce the heat a little and add the paste a bit at a time, stirring constantly. Boil for a few minutes to thicken the sauce, stirring occasionally.

Turn off the heat, and stir in the harissa.

Place the vegetables in the sterilized jar(s) and pour the spicy vinegar over. Seal immediately.

PICKLED BLACKBERRIES

Or should that say, 'blackberry vinegar'? Two glorious delights are yours for almost no effort: this is all about the spices and time. Don't be tempted to pour the vinegar over the fruit while it is still hot – a better texture and flavour result if the vinegar is cold. I've made this with a number of spice combinations, and this is my favourite, but do experiment as you wish: star anise, Ethiopian passion berries, lemon verbena leaves and bay are great alternatives. Once the berries are eaten, use the vinegar for dressings.

Fills 1 x 750ml (1½ pint) jar

250ml (9fl oz) cider vinegar
250ml (9fl oz) water
8 tbsp sugar
3 tbsp salt
6 verbena berries
6 juniper berries
3 allspice berries
10 Sichuan peppercorns
300g (10oz) blackberries

Pour the vinegar, water, sugar and salt into a medium pan and warm over a low–medium heat, stirring occasionally to dissolve the salt and sugar. Use a mortar and pestle to pound the spices just enough to break them open. Add the spices to the pan and simmer for 10 minutes. Remove from the heat and allow to cool.

Place the berries in a jar and pour the almost-cold spiced vinegar over. (Depending on the shape of your vessel and size of your berries there may be a little leftover liquid.) Seal and store somewhere out of direct sunlight. The pickled blackberries are best after a minimum of a fortnight.

SPICED NECTARINE JAM

Almost all I make of this goes on porridge rather than scones or toast, and for that I blame my daughter. It is a simple jam to make: the setting point is best gauged using a kitchen thermometer or by dropping a few drops on to a very cold plate and seeing if it wrinkles when pushed with a finger. In practice, you can just tell with this one as there is a sudden shift in consistency. Err on the cautious side: too much simmering and it will become too thick. The choice of pepper has a real influence on the jam: Timur berries have quite an upfront grapefruit flavour, but Sichuan pepper or an excellent quality black pepper work differently well. Adding the pepper just before jarring keeps its bright punctuation, rather than becoming infused into the whole.

Makes about 450ml (1 pint)
200g (7oz) sugar
160ml (5 ½ fl oz) water
8 nectarines, stoned
juice of 1 lemon
juice of 2 limes
½ whole star anise, freshly ground
½ lantern of mace (or 3 blades), freshly ground
8 Timur berries, freshly, coarsely ground

In a medium pan over a low–medium heat, bring the sugar and water to a simmer. Grate 2 of the nectarines into the syrup and add the lemon and lime juice. Simmer for 5 minutes. Add the star anise and mace and simmer until a little thicker.

Chop the remaining nectarines into 6–8mm (¼–½ in) dice and stir into the jam. Boil until the setting point has been reached. Remove from the heat, stir the Timur berries through and pour into sterilized jar(s) while still warm, then seal.

TOMATO AND VANILLA COMPOTE

If you haven't tried it, you may well be suspicious of the marriage of tomato and vanilla; let this be the bridge over the moat of doubt. This is somewhere between a jam and a compote, and is perfectly sweet without being cloying. Don't tell the person who's trying it that it has vanilla and likely as not they won't spot it until you say, and then be incredulous they didn't as it is peculiarly apparent. This is wonderful with goat's cheese on crostini, on burgers at a barbecue, with pasta and with roasted vegetables. You could make a salsa using the spirit of this: all raw, omit the oil, sugar and vinegar and add much coriander (cilantro) leaf.

**Makes about 500ml
(1 pint)**

60ml (4 tbsp) olive oil

3 large shallots, finely chopped

1 garlic clove, finely chopped

½ vanilla pod

600g (1lb 5oz) cherry tomatoes, cut into 1cm (½in) cubes

2 tbsp caster (superfine) sugar

1 tsp salt

80ml (3fl oz) Sauvignon Blanc vinegar

1 tsp Aleppo pepper

juice of ½ lime

freshly ground black pepper

Warm the oil in a medium-sized pan over a medium heat. Add the shallots, reduce the heat and cook for 10 minutes, stirring often. Add the garlic and cook for a minute. Split the vanilla pod, scrape the seeds loose and add them and the pod to the pan.

Add the tomatoes, sugar, salt and vinegar, and increase the heat until gently simmering. Cook slowly for 20 minutes, stirring often, until thickened.

Remove from the heat and stir in the Aleppo pepper and lime juice. Taste and adjust the seasoning as needed.

SAMBAL OELEK

Sambals are spicy, sour sauces and pastes of Indonesian origin that have spread and evolved over time; most have a lively combination of chilli, vinegar and salt at their heart. Embellishments around this central theme are many, but I think I love them best when down to their bare bones, as here. Piquín chillies – small, poky, and with a peculiar combination of citrus and nuttiness to their flavour – are perfect here, but do try other varieties. This will be more like a thin dressing than a paste. Try this in Lara Lee's sambal goreng tempe (page 170) and whenever a salty/sharp chilli kick is required.

Makes 40ml (1½fl oz)

10 dried Piquín chillies

30ml (2 tbsp) rice wine vinegar

5g (⅛oz) salt

Briefly whizz the chillies in a coffee grinder – I like to reduce them to coarse glitter rather than dust. Stir all the ingredients together thoroughly, or put into a jar, seal and shake to dissolve the salt.

MUSTARD SEED AND MINT RAITA

There is little more likely to be compromised by lack of care than the simplest of things. A few moments taken over raita is well rewarded in the pleasure it affords. The salting of the onion and the careful frying of the mustard seeds make such a difference. For once, this is where dried mint just wins for me, but feel free to use fresh mint if you prefer. Try this with the ajowan samosas (page 121).

Serves 4

½ small onion, very finely chopped

pinch of salt

juice of ½ lemon

1 tsp mustard seeds

1 tsp dried mint

200g (7oz) full-fat natural yoghurt

Rub a pinch of salt into the chopped onion and leave for 2 minutes. Rinse and drain, then stir in the lemon juice.

Dry-fry the mustard seeds in a small pan for 1 minute, until fragrant.

Stir everything into the yoghurt. Leave for 5 minutes before serving for the flavours to develop.

SRIRACHA

Sriracha – a salty, sour, sweet, garlicky hot sauce of Thai origin – has been adapted and adopted for good and ill as it has made its way around the world. Details are key to a good sriracha: a period of fermentation deepens and acidifies the flavour; the balance of different sugars gives richness without cloy; the rice vinegar has just the right balance of sourness and lightness. The proportion of salt is crucial too: 2% by weight of chillies and garlic ensures conditions in which only beneficial bacteria can proliferate. The fermentation time varies depending on the time of year and the heat of your kitchen, taking longer to ferment and produce small bubbles in cooler conditions. I've not been prescriptive about the variety or strength of the chillies, as this is very much to your taste. I often use habaneros as whatever their heat they have a fruitiness I love. If in doubt, go mild and adjust the heat with chilli powder at the end.

Makes 700ml (1 ½ pints)

450g (1lb) red chillies

8 garlic cloves, peeled but left whole

about 9g (⅓oz) sea salt

60g (2 ¼oz) caster (superfine) sugar

40g (1 ½oz) light muscovado sugar

4 tbsp rice vinegar

2 tbsp fish sauce (optional)

Slice off and discard the stalk from each chilli. Weigh the chillies and garlic and then measure out 2% of their combined weight in salt for the recipe.

Put all but the vinegar and fish sauce in a blender and whizz into a smoothish sauce. Decant into a sterilized jar and seal. Allow to ferment for 3–7 days, lifting the lid once a day to release any pressure from the CO_2 generated by fermentation.

Pour the sauce into a pan, stir in the vinegar and fish sauce (if using) and bring to a simmer over a medium heat. Cook, stirring often, for 5 minutes, tasting and tweaking the sweet and salt if required.

Pour into a sterilized jar or bottle and seal. Refrigerate once opened. Keeps for a few months at least.

PEPPER KOLA WITH GRAINS OF PARADISE... NO, RATHER WITH ALLIGATOR PEPPERS
by Yemisi Aribisala

The driver of the Margaret Ekpo International Airport shuttle took a shortcut in Calabar municipality, which turned into a slow crawl in a narrow back street where children peddled glossy green garden-eggs (a variety of aubergine/eggplant) in trays balanced on their heads. A lady in the shuttle asked the driver to buy her ₦100 garden eggs and ₦50 roasted groundnuts through his window. It was curiosity that made me ask for the same; that and I suppose ravenous hunger.

I despised garden eggs, and classified all of them – white, yellow, turmeric, green – as bitter and gritty. It was rare that I was so hungry, but I was ... and hoped that the groundnuts would take the edge off the taste of the garden eggs. I bit into a garden egg. There was just a suggestion of bitterness and a louder volume of organic sweetness. The texture was slight resistance in the smooth skin of the garden eggs followed by crunchiness and an aftertaste as refreshing as cucumbers. The groundnuts were obviously roasted that day, salty, spreading savouriness and a satisfying balance of sweet, bitter, fresh, savoury ... I was immediately converted.

Shortcuts can be problematic especially when they lead into traffic jams in narrow streets, and here I am battling one that exists in principle – in London where something called peanut butter has close to a hundred different brands that one can buy online and in supermarkets. There is nothing like peanut butter in Nigerian cuisine. You can surely buy something imported from the supermarket that has that label but what we have is Pepper Kola, which when broken down is roughly equal to roasted groundnuts with different spices.

Pepper Kola has no kola nut in it. The word kola is used (in a general sense) for what one uses to welcome guests. And this particular Pepper Kola is served at weddings and when esteemed guests come round. It is most likely still made entirely by hand.

Here is my long route recipe (overleaf).

Makes 4 as a snack

250g (9oz) raw peanuts

30 grains of paradise or
20–30 alligator peppers

50g (2oz) egusi (bitter
melon) or pumpkin seeds

1cm (½in) fresh ginger

½ tsp ground Cameroonian
pepper

Roast the peanuts in a dry pan over a low heat, moving them around until you can smell freshly baked biscuits and the peanut doesn't pull at your teeth when you bite into it (weird description, I know).

Wake up the grains of paradise or alligator peppers by rolling them around in the hot, dry pan. Alligator peppers swell and release a gingery aroma. They grow fatter too. Take them off the heat and let them cool.

Toast the egusi or pumpkin seeds until they pop and brown slightly. Allow both the peanuts and egusi/pumpkin seeds to cool only slightly, not completely, otherwise they are fiddly and jump out of the mortar.

Put all the ingredients into a mortar and work them with the pestle with a pound and slide motion that releases the oil from the nuts. You are aiming for the consistency of peanut butter. Traditionally the end product is cut with oil but I find this unnecessary. Sometimes calabash nutmeg is added to the spices.

Serve a dab of this with quartered garden eggs (aubergine/eggplant) or cucumber lengths.

MUHAMARRA

I first ate this Turkish/Syrian delight courtesy of Christine McFadden, author of the excellent book *Pepper*, and I have been making incarnations of it ever since. It is the sort of recipe that lends itself to inquisitive experimentation – less bread, different nuts, a tweak in the spices: this is how I make it at the moment. You can make it using a food processor, but I find the result a little too smooth.

Aleppo pepper – from the city close to the Syrian/Turkish border – is the authentic choice, and very good it is too, but sometimes I like paprika. Whichever I choose, I prefer it dusted on top rather than mixed in, as it allows the smokiness of the charred peppers to stay deep and unadulterated, and the layer of pepper/paprika to dance on the tongue.

I love this equally with crudités and flatbreads, especially the himbasha on (page 108).

Serves 4 generously as a dip

75g (2½oz) walnuts (or hazelnuts)

3 large red (bell) peppers

1 garlic clove, finely chopped

2 slices of white bread, whizzed into breadcrumbs

3 tbsp olive oil, plus extra for drizzling

1 tbsp tahini

1 tsp ground cumin

juice of ½ lemon

2 tbsp pomegranate molasses, plus extra for drizzling

1 tbsp Aleppo chilli flakes or ½ tsp paprika

sea salt

Preheat the oven to 180°C/350°F/gas mark 4.

Toast the walnuts on a baking sheet for 6–8 minutes until lightly golden. Allow them to cool.

Place the peppers in the flame of a gas hob for 15 minutes or so, using tongs to turn them until the skins of each are blackened. Place the peppers in a bowl, cover and allow to cool until handle-able. Use a sharp knife to scrape as much of the skin off as possible, then cut out and discard the core and stalk as well as the skin and seeds.

Using a mortar and pestle or food processor, blend everything except the Aleppo pepper/paprika together until semi-smooth.

Spoon into a bowl, smooth with a spoon, drizzle with a little more pomegranate molasses and olive oil, then sprinkle with Aleppo pepper/paprika.

KECAP MANIS

This Indonesian sweet, aromatic soy sauce is really something. Use it once and you'll find ideas about where to deploy it Catherine-wheeling out of your imagination. I rarely stir-fry pak choi without it; it tightens up the smoky michelada on page 256 perfectly; it brings rich character to a salad dressing and – peculiar as it sounds – I love it on ice cream. This might usually be made with a little molasses, but I prefer the flavour of half light muscovado, half white caster sugar. I also favour this sauce just on the thin side: bear in mind it will thicken as it cools.

Makes about 400ml (14fl oz)

200ml (7fl oz) soy sauce

175g (6oz) sugar

5 garlic cloves, bashed open

good thumb of fresh ginger, peeled and thinly sliced

2 whole star anise

1 clove

1 lantern of mace

2 allspice berries

1 tsp coriander seeds

Place everything in a pan and bring to the boil over a medium heat, stirring occasionally. Reduce the heat and simmer for 10 minutes or so, until it thickens a little. Allow to cool and infuse.

Decant, through a sieve set over a funnel, into a sterilized bottle, then seal. Store in the fridge. Keeps indefinitely.

BROWN SAUCE

Of the means by which we split people into two camps – Paul or John, smooth or crunchy, cream before jam or lunatic – red or brown sauce might be the most accurate determinant of those who we ought (and ought not) to spend time with. Here, for those of saucy right mind, is the best upgrade on that tangy, sweet-sharp sauce of the shops. Enjoy with chips, eggs and most definitely with sausages. Choice of pepper has a surprising impact: for me it has to be white pepper, and ideally white sarawak pepper.

Makes about 900ml (2 pints)

1 tbsp olive oil

1 large onion, finely chopped

2 tsp salt

400g (14oz) can chopped tomatoes

2 cooking apples, peeled, cored and chopped

8 dried apricots, chopped

8 prunes, chopped

3 garlic cloves

good thumb of fresh ginger, peeled and chopped

250ml (9fl oz) water

2 allspice berries

5 juniper berries

1 dried Mulato chilli

1 whole star anise

3 cloves

1 tbsp fennel seeds

6 white peppercorns

1 good lantern of mace

1 bay leaf

100ml (3½fl oz) red wine vinegar

30g (1oz) soft dark brown sugar

4 tbsp tamarind pulp

Heat the oil in a frying pan over a medium heat. Add the onion and 1 teaspoon of the salt and cook until soft and translucent: this should take 15–20 minutes.

Put the tomatoes, apples, dried fruit, onion, garlic and ginger into a large pan with the water. Slowly bring to the boil, then reduce to a gentle simmer. Cover and cook for 30 minutes, stirring occasionally.

Add the remaining ingredients and simmer, uncovered, for 50 minutes until it has thickened a little. Allow to cool for 10 minutes, before blending thoroughly. Immediately transfer to a sterilized jar or bottle and seal. Refrigerate once opened. Keeps for at least 3 months.

SOUTHERN STATES BARBECUE SAUCE

This is exactly the sort of barbecue sauce you might find on a sunny day get-together in the southern States where Kansas, Missouri, Tennessee and Arkansas rub up against each other. Sweet, sharp, poky and full of life, it is so good with pulled pork, hot dogs, burgers and ribs (page 98). Garlic powder might be more authentic than fresh but I'm not a huge fan; by all means use a teaspoon in place of the fresh garlic if you prefer. The chilli flakes should be to your preference of heat and flavour; I've gone for chipotle for its wonderful smokiness, as I tend to use this as much indoors as near the glowing coals of a barbecue.

Makes about 600ml (1¼ pints)

250ml (9fl oz) water

250ml (9fl oz) tomato ketchup

70g (2½oz) soft dark brown sugar

2 tbsp caster (superfine) sugar

2 tbsp molasses

80ml (3fl oz) cider vinegar

1 tbsp onion powder

2 garlic cloves, finely chopped

1 tsp ground cloves

2 tsp chipotle chilli flakes, ground

1 tbsp freshly ground black pepper

1 tbsp Worcestershire sauce

1 tsp salt

1 tsp celery seeds

Tip everything into a medium-sized pan and bring to a simmer. Stir and cook gently for 20–25 minutes, stirring occasionally, until a little thickened. Remove from the heat and decant into a sterilized bottle. Should keep for at least a fortnight in the fridge.

SAFFRON AIOLI

You could slather my dog's bed in aioli and I'd be tempted to eat it. Even writing this recipe makes me long for hot chips, panisse (page 112) or bourride (page 163). This is a good recipe to adapt: white pepper or Sichuan pepper instead of black, a pinch of ground cumin or maybe a little paprika, and while the saffron isn't essential, I do love its soft bitter hello.

Makes about 450ml (1 pint)

2 egg yolks

6 garlic cloves, crushed to a paste with a pinch of salt

100ml (3½fl oz) extra virgin olive oil

300ml (10fl oz) sunflower oil

few drops of white wine vinegar, to taste

pinch of saffron, soaked in a splash of warm water

sea salt and freshly ground black pepper

Whisk the egg yolks, a big pinch of salt, the garlic and a little pepper in a bowl.

Put both oils into a jug that is easy to pour from, then add a few drops of oil into the egg mix, whisking constantly to amalgamate, before adding the next drops. Once the mayonnaise is emulsified and holds its shape, you can add the oil in a thin stream while whisking.

Taste and check the seasoning, adding a few drops of vinegar, salt and a generous amount of freshly ground pepper. Finally whisk through the saffron and its soaking water.

Store in the fridge and use within a few days.

OLIO SANTO

'Oil of the saints' indeed. This is such a great oil to make, and I keep a bottle on the go for using as a dip for good bread, in dressings and drizzled where its aromatic punch is welcome. A slick of this coating a plain salad of butterhead lettuce is so special. Using quality ingredients has the effect of them all singing clearly, rather than any being lost in the fug of a cheap infusion. This is the perfect place for voatsiperifery – a gorgeous, rare pepper with a gentle citrus, warm, woody flavour – and korerima, which carries much of cardamom's familiar flavour with a sweet pepperiness. By all means experiment with other pepper varieties, fresh chilli, lemon thyme instead of bay, and so on.

Makes about 500ml (1 pint)

1 tsp voatsiperifery peppercorns

1 tsp white peppercorns

1 tsp Ethiopian korerima, or seeds from 4 green cardamom pods

generous pinch of salt

1 tsp Aleppo pepper

1 bay leaf, torn

1 garlic clove, sliced in half

500ml (1 pint) extra virgin olive oil

Place the first four ingredients into a mortar and pestle and gently crush the seeds; the salt will help everything bite. Add this, the Aleppo pepper, bay and garlic to a sterilized bottle and pour in the oil. Seal the bottle.

Although the oil will be good after a day of infusing, leave it for 3 weeks and it will become exceptional. Invert daily to encourage the flavours to be imparted.

ANISE AND NIGELLA REMOULADE

This side dish of French origin has many variations around the world; in the Southern States of the USA you can expect a little colour and heat from cayenne, in France mustard will likely add warmth, and in Scandinavia – where it is often served to top roast beef open sandwiches or with fried fish – a pinch of curry powder and/or turmeric might bring earthiness and colour. I like this just on the dry side; by all means add a little more crème fraîche if you are the slippery sort.

Serves 4

1 celeriac (600–700g/1¼–1½lb), peeled and cut into very thin matchsticks, or coarsely grated

juice of 1 lemon

200g (7oz) crème fraîche

2 tbsp Dijon mustard

1 tsp anise seed

1 tsp nigella seeds

good pinch each of sea salt and freshly ground black pepper

As you prepare the celeriac, toss it in half the lemon juice to prevent it discolouring.

Mix all the remaining ingredients together in another bowl. Stir into the celeriac, then taste and adjust the seasoning if needed.

DILL HONEY MUSTARD DRESSING

This is based on my wife's recipe – a beautifully balanced sharp, sweet, punchy dressing – to which I occasionally add a tweak of spice to go with the mustard. Occasionally it's anise, sometimes celery seed, more often it's lightly toasted dill seed (crushed or ground). If you have made the mostarda di frutta (page 102), you can use a few spoons of that in place of the honey and mustard. Try this for dressing salad leaves or steamed greens; a pinch of chilli powder can be special with darker greens.

Makes 75ml (3fl oz)

1 tbsp apple cider vinegar

1 generous tsp smooth English mustard

1 generous tsp honey

½ tsp dill seeds, ground

good pinch each of sea salt and freshly ground black pepper

3 tbsp olive oil

Place everything but the oil in a jar, twist the lid on and shake it vigorously. Add the olive oil and shake until it forms an emulsion. Adjust the seasoning if needed.

CARAWAY YOGHURT DRESSING

Dressings are one of those times where using a fine quality of pepper will really make itself known. Once again, use this as a template for your own variations: coconut yoghurt, cider vinegar or lime juice, dill seed or khmeli-suneli instead of the caraway are all good places to start.

Makes about 225ml (8fl oz)
120g (4oz) natural yoghurt
3 tbsp white wine vinegar
2 tsp caraway seeds, lightly toasted in a dry pan
pinch each of sea salt and good freshly ground black pepper
3 tbsp olive oil

Place everything but the oil in a jar, twist the lid on and shake it vigorously. Add the olive oil and shake until it forms an emulsion. Taste and adjust the seasoning if needed.

ZA'ATAR VINAIGRETTE

This spicy, sour, punchy dressing goes as well with roasted vegetables as it does with plain lettuce leaves, punchier peppery leaves or even the darker iron-heavy kales and other greens of winter.

Makes 100ml (3½fl oz)
80ml (3fl oz) extra virgin olive oil
2 tbsp za'atar (page 72)
juice of 1 lime
1 tbsp Dijon mustard
salt

Place everything but the salt in a jar, twist the lid on and shake it vigorously until it forms an emulsion. Taste and add a pinch of salt if you think it needs it; depending on what it is dressing and your tastes.

MOSTARDA DI FRUTTA

This Italian speciality brings together the sweet/sour of fruit with the punch of the mustardy syrup so beautifully; if I'm not thinking about sausages to go with it when I make it, I'm thinking about salty cheese. The choice of fruit is yours: nectarines and peaches, grapes and quince are other favourites; I'm less keen on the citrus some include. Whichever fruit you choose should have a total prepared weight of 800g (1lb 12oz). Wine is a traditional addition to the syrup, but I love krupnik and ratafia too. The mustards bring punch but not too much: go for English mustard and/or more mustard powder if you want more.

Makes 1 litre (2 pints)

20 cherries, halved and stoned

4 plums, stoned and cut into wedges

3 kiwi fruit, peeled and cut into wedges

3 small figs, cut into wedges

2 pears, peeled, cored and cut into wedges

400g (14oz) caster (superfine) sugar

juice of 1 lemon

3 tbsp krupnik, ratafia (pages 252 and 254) or white wine

1 tsp mustard powder

3 tbsp Dijon mustard

1 tbsp yellow mustard seeds

1 tbsp black mustard seeds

1 bay leaf, torn

Place the fruit and sugar in a bowl and stir together. Leave for at least 12 hours, stirring gently halfway through. The sugar will have been made into syrup by the fruit juices; don't worry if some sugar is only semi-dissolved.

Set a colander over a medium pan, gently pour the syrupy fruit into the colander and allow to drain.

Add the remaining ingredients to the syrup in the pan. Bring to a simmer, stirring occasionally, and gently simmer for 15 minutes or so until slightly thickened. Remove from the heat and allow to cool for 10 minutes.

Spoon the fruit carefully into a sterilized jar, pour the warm syrup in, seal and allow to cool. Leave for a few days to allow the flavours to develop. Store in the fridge once open.

CAPE MALAY SPICED WALNUTS

This may not be an authentic or traditional use of this excellent spice blend, and I guess if I was after a little more of that I'd make this with macadamia nuts, as South Africa is the world's largest producer of them, but I love the way this clings to the walnuts' folds and canyons.

Makes a snack for 2 greedy people

2 tbsp soft light brown sugar

1 tbsp Cape Malay spice blend (page 61)

1 tsp sea salt

1 ½ tbsp olive oil

220g (8oz) walnuts

Preheat the oven to 170°C/340°F/gas mark 3 and lay a sheet of baking parchment on a baking sheet.

Mix the sugar, spice blend and salt in a large bowl. Warm the olive oil gently in a pan, then add the walnuts, coating them thoroughly.

Tip the nuts into the spiced sugar and toss to coat the nuts well. Spread evenly on the lined baking sheet and place in the oven. Cook for 10 minutes, checking after 7 minutes as they can catch. Tip into a bowl and grab an excellent drink.

SOUR CHILLI MELON

This is about the best way I know with melon. The sour chilli seasoning complements the sweet, ripe fruit perfectly, but the key components are not the actual ingredients but what they deliver: salt, sour and heat. If you don't have all the ingredients for the sour chilli seasoning, you can create a similar impression by using sumac or a little extra lime juice for sourness, sea salt and chilli flakes and/or pepper. Shichimi togarashi and Chinese five-spice are other special blends to try with lime and salt. This also works well with pineapple.

Serves 4

1 canteloupe melon

extra virgin olive oil, for drizzling

juice of ½ lime

1 tbsp sour chilli seasoning (page 70)

Cut the melon in half through the poles, scoop out any seeds, then cut each half into wedges. Remove the peel from each.

Arrange on a serving plate and drizzle with a little olive oil. Squeeze the lime juice over, sprinkle with sour chilli seasoning and serve.

NIGELLA AND AJOWAN PARATHAS

Once in a while, usually when the days are short, my daughter, wife and I make a curry each to enjoy in front of a large fire and an old film. These are the flatbreads I invariably turn to to accompany. I'm not sure there is such a thing as really bad parathas, but not all are born equal, it's true. Here, the ajowan and nigella Simon-and-Garfunkel to delightful effect.

Makes 4

250g (9oz) plain (all-purpose) flour, plus extra for dusting

salt

sugar

¼ tsp ajowan seeds

¾ tsp nigella seeds

70g (2½oz) butter or ghee, melted

150ml (5fl oz) water

Tip the flour into a medium bowl and stir in ½ teaspoon of salt, a pinch of sugar and the seeds. Rub in 2 tablespoons of the melted butter or ghee using your fingertips. Mix in the water to form a rough dough, then cover and leave for 5 minutes. Knead for a few minutes on a floured surface until the dough is smooth and elastic. Cover and leave to rest for 30 minutes.

Divide the dough into four equal-sized pieces. Roll out one piece into a circle about 20cm (8in) wide and brush with 1 teaspoon of melted butter or ghee. Roll the circle up then coil into a snail shape. Repeat with the remaining pieces of dough. Roll out each of the coiled snails on a floured surface into a circle a couple of millimetres thick and 20cm (8in) in diameter.

Heat a large frying pan or grill (broiler) until hot, then dry-fry each paratha for 1–2 minutes, or until parts of the top surface look cooked and the bottom is brown in patches. Flip the paratha over and cook until the bottom of the paratha begins to turn brown in patches and all traces of raw flour have disappeared. Brush with a little melted butter then wrap the paratha tightly in a clean tea towel to keep warm while you cook the remaining parathas.

HIMBASHA

Argued by some as being of Eritrean origin, this flatbread is widely appreciated as a celebration bread across the border in Ethiopia. Of the many variations, green cardamom is a constant, and I have to say I like it best paired with sultanas and black sesame in this classic sweet/savoury combination. Himbasha is especially good with hummus and muhamarra (page 93). Easy to make by hand or using a mixer.

Makes 1 large flatbread (to cut into 8)

275g (10oz) plain (all-purpose) flour

1 tsp active dry yeast

3 tbsp sugar

very generous pinch of salt

15 cardamom pods, seeds only, ground

2 tsp black sesame seeds

55g (2oz) sultanas (golden raisins)

8 tsp olive oil, plus a little extra to oil the tin

120ml (4fl oz) warm water

2 tbsp milk

Combine the flour, yeast, sugar, salt, ground cardamom and black sesame seeds. Stir in the sultanas and olive oil. Add the water and combine to form a soft dough. Knead until it has softened (for 8 minutes or so if doing by hand). Form into a circular disc, cover and allow to double in size. This should take about an hour, depending on the temperature of your kitchen.

Lightly oil a shallow 22cm (9in) cake or tart tin. Use your palms to shape the dough into a wide circle, place in the tin and use your fingers to press the dough across the base until it's covered. Cover and leave for 5 minutes. Press the dough back to the rim if it has shrunk back a little. Cover and leave for 40 minutes.

Preheat the oven to 170°C/340°F/gas mark 3.

Use the tip of a sharp knife to score a wheel/web pattern into the dough. Brush with milk and bake in the centre of the oven for 25 minutes until golden. Remove and allow to cool a little on a wire rack before serving.

PAN DE MUERTO

In early November, in the run-up to the Mexican Día de Muertos, or
'Day of the Dead', pan de muerto, or 'bread of the dead', is traditionally
eaten in celebration of those who have passed. Soft, sweet, infused with orange
and lightly spiced, it is welcome in my house at any time of year. The dough
is floppier than some and needs wet hands to remove the dough before shaping,
and floured hands for the shaping itself. Be gentle but bold. And while it's
cooking, make the tascalate on page 265.

Makes 1 bread

10g (⅓ oz) active dry yeast

150ml (5 fl oz) warm water

180g (6oz) caster (superfine)
sugar, plus a little extra to
sprinkle

100g (3½ oz) butter,
softened

2 tbsp olive oil

zest of 1 orange, finely
grated

2 good pinches of salt

1 tbsp orange blossom
water

2 tbsp anise seed

4 eggs

570g (1lb 4oz) plain
(all-purpose) flour

Mix the yeast, warm water and a pinch of the sugar in a small bowl. Leave
for 5 minutes.

In a large bowl, beat the sugar, butter, oil, orange zest, salt, orange blossom
water and anise seeds until light and fluffy. Lightly whisk the eggs in a cup,
then slowly add, beating continuously. Fold in the flour to form a soft dough.
Cover the bowl with a damp tea towel and leave somewhere warm to prove
for around 4 hours (check after 3), or until the dough has doubled in size.

Preheat the oven to 220°C/425°F/gas mark 7.

Place a piece of baking parchment on a baking sheet. Lightly flour a work
surface and – with wet hands – tip the dough on to it. Cut off around a
quarter of the dough and set aside; gently shape the larger portion into a
dome and place it on the baking sheet.

Use the quarter of dough to create a ball around 6cm (2½ in) across and four
dog bone shapes. Use a little water to stick the ball on the top of the dome –
like the bobble on a hat – and the dog bones running up to it from the base,
looking like a cross from above.

Bake for 5 minutes, then reduce the temperature to 160°C/320°F/gas mark 3.
Use a cake tester/cocktail stick to test after a further 25 minutes of cooking:
it can be a little variable and may need 10 minutes more before the stick comes
out clean. Sprinkle with caster sugar. Allow to cool on a wire rack.

PANISSE WITH LEMON THYME AND BERBERE

A couple of weeks ago I had lunch at the Sessions Arts Club in London and I've thought about it every day since. Myself and an old friend ate a lot. Every mouthful was extraordinary. The panisse has had me craving it daily, so this morning I made this interpretation and ate enough for four.

Essentially, panisse are beautifully nutty chips from the south of France; golden jengas of delight. Dusted in excellent salt they are delicious, but don't let that put you off going for more of a flourish. Here the bright resin of lemon thyme, the soft attack of cubeb pepper, and the lively warmth of berbere – an Ethiopian spice blend – make for something really special. Do try combinations of rosemary and sumac, sage and baharat, and orange thyme and garam masala too. You can do the steps up to the slicing and frying the day before if it suits.

Two things: any more than the approximate size of the dish isn't crucial as the panisse will just be a little thinner/thicker; make sure you cook and eat the skinny offcuts, as they are crisp delights.

Serves 4 as a snack

250g (9oz) chickpea (gram) flour

10 cubeb peppercorns, coarsely ground

1 tsp fine salt

1 tbsp olive oil, plus extra for oiling and frying

1 litre (2 pints) water

good sprig of lemon thyme, leaves only

a few very generous pinches of berbere (page 59)

coarse sea salt

Lightly oil a dish of 25 x 18cm (10 x 7in) internal dimensions.

Stir the pepper and salt through the flour, then add the flour, 1 tablespoon of oil and 300ml (10fl oz) of the water to a large pan and whisk until smooth. Whisk in the remaining 700ml (1½ pints) water. Bring to the boil over a medium heat, stirring often. Reduce the heat and whisk as the mixture thickens. After 10 minutes or so it will gradually begin to pull away from the side of the pan as you stir. Spoon the mix into the oiled dish, using a spatula to scrape everything from the pan and smooth the top as well as you can. Allow it to cool before placing in the fridge.

Preheat the oven to 130°C/260°F/gas mark ½.

Run a knife around the edge of the dish to release the sides, then turn out on to a chopping board. Slice across the short sides into pieces 2cm (¾in) wide. Turn each on its edge and slice off the uneven top edge.

Pour enough olive oil into a small or medium frying pan to come 1.5cm (⅝in) up the side, then set over a medium heat. Test if the oil is hot enough with a small piece of panisse offcut: it should sizzle away nicely when lowered into the oil with tongs.

Fry the panisse in small batches – four or so – to avoid crowding the pan, turning with tongs after 4–5 minutes when nicely golden. Once evenly cooked, use tongs to lift the panisse from the oil on to a plate lined with kitchen paper. Transfer to the oven to keep warm and repeat until all are cooked. Place on a serving dish and sprinkle with lemon thyme, berbere and coarse sea salt.

BAHARAT BLACKCURRANT ECCLES CAKES

What an advert for Anglo-Turkish harmony, with the classic northern England Eccles cake getting a generous spicing with baharat. The aromatic, earthy spiciness of the blend works so well with sweet/sharp blackcurrants, and it's a combination you can improvise around: sweet garam masala, or a blend of ground allspice and fennel, in place of the baharat; blueberries instead of the blackcurrants. I find this easiest to make with frozen currants (no need to defrost before cooking) as they are so much easier to top and tail with the scrape of a thumbnail.

Makes 6

20g (¾oz) unsalted butter

50g (2oz) soft light brown sugar, plus a little extra for sprinkling

1 tsp baharat (page 59)

80g (3oz) blackcurrants

1 sheet of ready-rolled puff pastry

2 egg whites, lightly beaten

yoghurt or cream, to serve

Preheat the oven to 180°C/350°F/gas mark 4.

Melt the butter in a small pan, remove from the heat and combine with the sugar and baharat. Stir in the blackcurrants.

Cut six 12cm (5in) circles in the pastry and spoon a little of the filling into the centre of each: you'll be surprised how little is enough. Pull up one side over to the other, covering the filling, and pinch together into a semicircle to seal. Repeat with all the circles.

Brush with egg white and sprinkle with a little sugar. Use a sharp knife to make three short slashes in the top of each, then transfer to a baking sheet. Bake for 15–18 minutes until golden brown.

Serve with yoghurt or whichever cream takes your fancy.

DUKKAH EGGS

A single fried egg can lace the shoe of a meal together like little else. It pairs with green succulence, crisp carbohydrates and spice to such excellent effect. Here, it turns a few simple ingredients into a seriously good set-you-up breakfast. Try this with griddled asparagus instead of bread, or even roasted carrots. I have this as often with boiled eggs as fried too.

Serves 2

1 tbsp olive oil

4 eggs

4 slices of sourdough, or
4 small flatbreads, toasted

dukkah (page 63), for
sprinkling

sea salt and freshly ground
black pepper

Heat the olive oil in a small frying pan over a medium heat until hot but not smoking. Crack one or two eggs into the oil and cook until bubbling and beginning to crisp around the edges. To cook the top of the yolk, cover the pan briefly. Lift the lid every 30 seconds or so, cooking the yolk until you get the desired doneness. Transfer the eggs to a plate.

Repeat with the remaining eggs, adding another teaspoon of oil if needed. Toast the bread lightly. Sprinkle dukkah generously over the eggs, season and serve on or beside the toast.

Pictured opposite.

POTTED CRAB

Having grown up used to extracting fish paste from a tall narrow glass jar with the tip of a knife to be scraped across charcoally Mother's Pride, I feel a special affection for this simple, perfect upgrade. The spice may seem little in quantity, but the mace and fenugreek conspire to lift the crab beautifully. If you are without mace, try nutmeg: it will be differently superb. The type of crabmeat is your choice: I prefer half white, half brown.

Serves 4

150g (5oz) unsalted butter

good pinch of ground mace

pinch of chilli flakes

pinch of ground fenugreek

1 small bay leaf

200g (7oz) crabmeat

1 lemon

sea salt and freshly ground
black pepper

toast, to serve

Simmer the butter in a pan with the mace, chilli flakes, fenugreek and bay leaf for 2 minutes. Remove from the heat and cool the mixture until it is room temperature.

Add the crabmeat and stir well, then season with salt, pepper and lemon juice to taste. Fill four ramekins, small jars or cups with the mixture or spoon it into a bowl.

Either serve straight away or keep in the fridge for a day, removing from the fridge 30 minutes before serving.

Serve with hot toast and the remaining lemon cut into wedges.

SAUERKRAUT FRITTERS WITH CARAWAY SEEDS
by Irina Georgescu

In Romania we don't use a lot of spices; we keep things simple and use black pepper and paprika. Caraway seeds are more common in Transylvania, and once you cross the Carpathian mountains into other regions, you will rarely see them. I have found in old books, and by listening to podcasts related to Romanian cuisine, that up until the 19th century, saffron, ginger and cinnamon were also used in savoury dishes. They completely disappeared from our recipes when paprika (boia in Romanian) started to gain in popularity, although cinnamon appears in sweet dishes only. Here is a delicious recipe where paprika and caraway work wonderfully together.

This is a Romanian pantry dish, since it's prepared with staple ingredients that are found in most Romanian homes. We love fermented foods and pickles, and use them not only as side dishes, but as the star ingredients in more substantial courses or in tangy, moreish snacks. Mum would prepare these fritters from leftover sauerkraut, or from the leaves that were not quite perfect for making sarmale *(stuffed sauerkraut leaves). We ferment cabbages whole in Romania, using the same method as for sauerkraut, whether with salt only or with brine. In this way, the leaves soften, gain more flavour (and are more nutritious), and they are very easy to roll. However, not all of them pass the eagle eye of the cook, looking for the thin-crunchy perfect leaf with no holes. It's a tall order, since the cabbages are pressed and squeezed together in wooden barrels, fermenting and melting together. The rejected leaves are put to a good use in dishes such as a ciorba – a broth with potatoes and smoked ham – or baked layers of sauerkraut and mincemeat or sausages, or sauerkraut with duck legs. One of the quickest dishes to make is a sort of fritter or pancake. There are two versions: the one given here, and the other, where you make a pancake batter and dip small clusters of sauerkraut into the batter and fry them.*

The usual pairings with sauerkraut are caraway seeds and fresh dill, plus sour cream on top and pickled green chilli peppers; trust me, it works. These fritters are a snack, or you can serve them with potatoes mashed with sour cream and dill.

Serves 4 as a snack

10g (⅓oz) caraway seeds

350g (12oz) sauerkraut, well drained

80g (3oz) chopped white onion

1 egg, beaten

30g (1oz) plain (all-purpose) flour

2 tsp sweet paprika

½ tsp freshly ground black pepper

sunflower oil, for frying

For the dip

Try the mustard seed and mint raita on page 88 with 1 tsp dill seed instead of the mustard seed

Tip the caraway seeds into a dry frying pan and heat over a medium–high heat for 3–4 minutes until lightly toasted. Tip into a bowl with all the remaining ingredients, except the oil, and mix together.

Heat a thin layer of oil in a frying pan over a medium heat.

Use a tablespoon to get even-sized fritters, scoop and shape each fritter in the palm of your hand, giving it a slightly elongated shape. Place the fritters in the pan, a few at a time, and fry until golden brown, gently pressing on top and turning them on each side a couple of times. This will take 5–6 minutes. Drain the fritters on kitchen paper and repeat with the remaining mixture. Serve immediately.

AJOWAN SAMOSAS

Exhibit A in the case for the irresistibility of pastry, spice and frying. The flavours jostling for attention here sing as a choir rather than compete at another's expense, though it is ajowan that holds the whole together. Make these once and eat them finger-tinglingly hot and dusted in chaat and you'll find it hard to eat them from anywhere else but your kitchen.

Makes 8

250g (9oz) floury potatoes, peeled and chopped into 2cm (¾in) cubes

225g (8oz) plain (all-purpose) flour, plus extra for dusting

1 tsp nigella seeds

1 tsp ajowan seeds

4 tbsp vegetable or sunflower oil, plus extra for shallow-frying

100ml (3½fl oz) water

1 red onion, finely chopped

1 medium carrot, peeled and coarsely grated

2 garlic cloves, finely chopped

2 tsp cumin seeds

½–1 tsp chilli flakes

200g (7oz) frozen peas, defrosted

1 tsp garam masala (page 64)

sea salt

1 tsp chaat masala (page 62), to serve

Boil the potatoes for 10 minutes or so until just tender, then drain and cool.

Mix the flour, nigella seeds, ajowan seeds, 2 tablespoons of the oil, the water and ½ teaspoon of salt to form a dough. Knead until smooth, cover and leave to one side.

Heat the remaining 2 tablespoons of oil in a frying pan and fry the onion, carrot and garlic with the cumin seeds and chilli flakes for 15 minutes until soft and just beginning to brown. Roughly mash the potato, then mix with the carrot and onion mixture, the peas, the garam masala and salt to taste.

Divide the samosa dough into 4 equal pieces then roll each piece into a smooth ball. Roll each ball into a thin round about 18cm (7in) in diameter and a few millimetres thick, then cut these in half to make two semicircles. Take a semicircle of dough, wet the straight edge with water and then make into a cone by overlapping either end of the straight edge and pinching to seal.

Fill the cone with a couple of tablespoons of samosa filling, then wet the top edges and pinch together to seal. Leave on a floured surface and repeat with the remaining semicircles.

Carefully heat 2cm (¾in) of oil in a high-sided frying pan. The oil is ready when you drop a small piece of the dough into the oil and it sizzles and floats to the surface. Fry the samosas for 2 minutes, or until golden brown all over (you may need to do this in batches) then drain on kitchen paper. Sprinkle with the chaat masala to serve.

ADVIEH STUFFED AUBERGINES

I know of no better indicator of whether you need to get out more than if you have the time or inclination to stuff a marrow. This applies to a lesser degree to most vegetables: aubergines are the happiest of exceptions, and in advieh – an Iranian coming together of dried rose petals, cardamom, cumin, cinnamon and other variables – it finds a perfect partner.

Serves 4

80g (3oz) basmati rice

80g (3oz) red lentils

4 aubergines (eggplants), cut in half widthways, flesh scooped out and finely chopped

2 tbsp olive oil

2 onions, coarsely grated

1 garlic clove, finely chopped

1 tbsp advieh (page 59)

100g (3½oz) tomato passata, or chopped tomatoes

2 tbsp tomato purée (paste)

50g (2oz) raisins

300ml (10fl oz) water

2 tbsp pine nuts or flaked (slivered) almonds

25g (1oz) parsley, finely chopped

sea salt and freshly ground black pepper

Preheat the oven to 140°C/280°F/gas mark 1.

Bring a large pan of water to the boil, add the rice, lentils and finely chopped aubergine and boil, uncovered, for 7 minutes. Drain well.

Meanwhile, heat the olive oil in a large pan and fry the onion, garlic and advieh over a low heat for 10–15 minutes, or until soft. Spoon half this mixture into a bowl, add the drained lentil mixture and put to one side.

Add the passata, tomato purée, raisins and ½ teaspoon of salt to the onion mix in the pan and cook for 5 minutes until thickened. Add the water and bring to the boil, then remove from the heat and season with salt and pepper.

Stuff the lentil mixture into the hollowed-out aubergine halves. Spoon the sauce into a small roasting dish then place the aubergines on top of the sauce. Cover tightly with foil and cook in the oven for 1½–2 hours until very soft.

Sprinkle with the pine nuts or flaked almonds and parsley and serve, perhaps with yoghurt or raita on the side.

BAHARAT CAULIFLOWER

In Istanbul, the Middle Eastern spice blend baharat might contain dried mint; in Tunis it might be laden with cinnamon: wherever and however, it should be fiery, fragrant and floral. Here, the unchallenging, welcoming character of the cauliflower allows every element to sing. By all means roast or fry the cauliflower if you prefer.

Serves 2 as a main, 4 as a side

2 tbsp tahini

150g (5oz) natural yoghurt

1 large garlic clove, crushed to a paste with a little salt

juice of ½ lemon

1 large firm cauliflower, leaves and stalk trimmed

1 tbsp olive oil

4 tsp baharat (page 59), plus extra for sprinkling

small handful of coriander (cilantro) leaves

generous scattering of chilli flakes

sea salt and freshly ground black pepper

Blend the tahini, yoghurt, garlic and lemon juice to a smooth sauce with a big pinch each of salt and pepper. Put to one side. Preheat the grill (broiler) to high.

Cut 4 thick slices from the middle of the cauliflower and keep the rest to eat later. Brush both sides with the oil, season with salt, pepper and half the baharat. Lay them on a baking sheet.

Grill (broil) under a high heat for 2–3 minutes until the cauliflower starts to brown. Flip over and do the same on the other side. Serve on top of the tahini sauce, sprinkled with coriander and chilli flakes and a little more baharat.

STAR ANISE PAK CHOI

The trebling up of star anise – powdered, whole and in the kecap manis sauce – is so good here, with its implied sweetness (as well as that of the sauce) contrasting beautifully with the squeaky pak choi. Every week I find something new this complements, but sausages and oily fish are hard to beat.

Serves 4 as a side

2 tbsp sesame oil

4 pak choi, quartered lengthways

1 whole star anise, half ground to a powder, half intact

3 tbsp kecap manis (page 94)

juice of 1 lime

juice of 1 lemon

sea salt and freshly ground black pepper

Heat the sesame oil in a wok over a lively flame. Add the pak choi and the intact half of star anise and stir-fry, agitating around the pan with a large metal spoon. Season with salt and pepper. As the leafy ends start to wilt and the core takes on a little colour, add the kecap manis, tossing the pak choi to coat. Cook for a minute longer, then pour in the citrus juices. Cook for a minute or two to reduce the liquid a little. Season again and serve, dusting with the star anise powder.

SPICED SWEETCORN

I eat more sweetcorn with every year that passes and, along with barbecued sweetcorn with lime and chilli, this may be my favourite way with it. The marinade here does so much for the flavour of the dish but as with the painter following on from the plasterer and getting all the credit, the chaat makes a late appearance and steals the glory. For the chutney, try and get everything as finely chopped as possible.

Serves 6

6 corn corbs

2 tsp chaat masala (page 62)

For the green chutney

½ small red onion, very finely chopped

big pinch of salt

20g (¾oz) bunch of mint, leaves picked and finely chopped

20g (¾oz) bunch of coriander (cilantro), finely chopped

2 long green chillies, finely chopped

1 tsp caster (superfine) sugar

juice of 1 lemon

For the marinade

2 tsp Kashmiri chilli powder, or use 1 tsp chilli and 1 tsp paprika

½ tsp ground turmeric

1 tsp ground cumin

1 tsp ground coriander

100g (3½oz) natural yoghurt

1 tsp grated fresh ginger

2 garlic cloves, crushed

sea salt and freshly ground black pepper

Rub the big pinch of salt into the red onion, then rinse, drain and put to one side.

Boil the corn cobs in a large pan of salted water for 5 minutes until just tender, then drain well (reserving the water) and pat dry.

Mix the ingredients for the marinade together, coat the corn with half the mixture and set aside to marinate.

Mix most of the salted red onion with the remaining chutney ingredients and put to one side while you heat the barbecue (grill) or grill (broiler) to medium–high.

Grill the corn cobs for 5–10 minutes until lightly charred, turning frequently, and brushing with the remaining marinade.

Sprinkle the sweetcorn with chaat masala, spoon over the green chutney and scatter with the remaining onion.

SPROUT AND SPRING ONION KIMCHI

Kimchi is a classic, delicious ferment of Korean origin, that while traditionally made with Chinese cabbage, takes beautifully to other leafy vegetables. The constants are the fiery sauce and the 2% salt-to-vegetable ratio. Many recipes call for shrimp paste as well as the fish sauce but this is a step too far down the funky fishy road for me; by all means add it, but be prepared for the pot of leftover shrimp paste to make you aware of its presence even when well sealed, inside a bag, in a cupboard, surrounded in a concrete bunker 200ft below ground level and 3 miles from your house.

This is good as a side, but do try it in an omelette or in place of the sauerkraut in the fritters on page 119.

Fills a 700ml (1 ½ pint) jar

800g (1lb 12oz) Brussels sprouts

6 large spring onions (scallions)

about 16g (½oz) fine sea salt

2 garlic cloves, finely chopped

5cm (2in) fresh ginger, peeled and finely chopped

2 tbsp gochugaru (Korean chilli flakes)

2 tsp fish sauce

Remove the outer leaves of the sprouts and any rough outer and the coarsest green parts of the spring onions. Weigh the sprouts and onions: measure out 2% of their combined weight in salt for the recipe.

Finely shred the sprouts and spring onions and place in a large bowl. Add the salt and rub thoroughly through. Allow everything to soften for an hour or so and form a little brine.

In a small cup, make a paste by combining the garlic, ginger, chilli flakes and fish sauce.

Drain the vegetables in a colander, retaining the brine in a bowl beneath. In a large bowl, stir the paste through the vegetables, adding a little of the brine to loosen the mix. Spoon the kimchi into a sterilized jar, pressing down well to exclude air bubbles. I use a freezer bag part-filled with water to keep the vegetables submerged, although you can also use a pickle pebble, if you have one. Seal the jar.

Allow the kimchi to ferment for 5 days at room temperature. Taste it: it should be pleasingly sour. It may take longer to reach this point in a cool kitchen; leave it as long as you fancy until it reaches a flavour you like. When it is ready, transfer it to the fridge to slow fermentation to a virtual standstill.

SEEDY SPROUT SLAW

Along with lamb chops, trifle, mulberries, lardy cake and salty roast chicken skin, I can never have too many sprouts. Roasted, fried, steamed, buttered, whatever: this is one of my favourite ways with them. It is a hugely versatile slaw; a teaspoon of black mustard seeds, fennel seeds, or a good pinch of garam masala all work beautifully. I'm sure you'll think of more. This is easiest if you have a food processor that has a slicing attachment, but otherwise take your time over the thinness of slice. And use as much or as little of the dressing as you fancy; I vary it depending on what it's accompanying.

Serves 4

1 tbsp poppy seeds

2 tbsp pumpkin seeds

caraway yoghurt dressing (page 101)

400g (14oz) Brussels sprouts, peeled and thinly sliced

3 apples, thinly sliced

½ large red onion, thinly sliced

2 celery sticks, thinly sliced

1 tbsp Aleppo pepper

sea salt and freshly ground black pepper

Toast the seeds in a dry pan over a medium heat to release their flavour, shaking the pan occasionally to prevent burning.

Spoon half of the caraway dressing into the bottom of a large bowl along with the seeds and a generous pinch each of salt and pepper. Add the sprouts, apple, onion and celery and toss everything until well coated. Add a little more dressing if you prefer. Scatter the Aleppo pepper over and serve.

TEMPERO BAIANO CABBAGE

If the oven has been roasting a meaty main course, pop this in to cook while it rests. The cabbage goes in so neat and tight, and comes out looking five gins in, but man does it taste good. I love the intense mix of spice and herbs that this Brazilian spice blend brings, but you should try this with chaat masala, panch phoran, hawaij, or whatever takes your fancy.

Serves 4

1 pointed green cabbage

2 tbsp olive oil

2–3 tsp tempero baiano (page 71)

sea salt

squeeze of lime, to serve

Preheat the oven to 200°C/400°F/gas mark 6.

Cut the cabbage from top to tail into four or six wedges, depending on the size of the cabbage. Lay the wedges on a tray and drizzle with olive oil, turning each quarter so its cut side is uppermost to encourage oil into the folds. Salt generously, then sprinkle the tempero baiano onto each cut side.

Roast in the oven for 15 minutes or so. It should be burnt here and there. Serve with a squeeze of lime.

SMASHED KIMCHI CUCUMBER

A couple of years ago I ate something approximating this in a restaurant in London. That much is all my cloudy memory will recall. In the absence of more details dropping like reels on the fruit machine into my mind, I have taken to my own re-creation. I love the flavours of kimchi and this is very much a tribute to them, without the wait that making kimchi requires: the vinegar offers the sourness that fermenting usually provides. You could slice the cucumbers but the roughly smashed edges encourage the flavours into the flesh.

Serves 4 as a side

2 large cucumbers, peeled

generous pinch of salt

1 tbsp rice vinegar

1 tbsp Shaoxing rice wine

1 garlic clove, finely chopped

3cm (1in) fresh ginger, peeled and finely chopped

1 tbsp sesame oil

1 tbsp gochugaru (Korean chilli flakes)

1 tsp fish sauce

1 tsp granulated sugar

small handful of coriander (cilantro), sliced

Slice the cucumbers lengthways, then each half into four pieces. With the cut side face down on a chopping board, and one hand preventing the cucumber piece skating cross the kitchen, use your knuckles to press into the back of the cucumber pieces with just enough pressure to lightly smash them a little.

Add all but the cucumbers and coriander to a bowl and stir vigorously to incorporate thoroughly. Pat the cucumber pieces dry using a clean tea towel, then add them to the bowl and toss until thoroughly coated. Allow to rest and soak in the flavours for 5 minutes before serving.

Serve on a platter, sprinkled with the coriander.

GUNPOWDER POTATOES

I spend what some might see as a peculiar amount of time pondering what my desert island/pre-firing squad meal would be. The highly seasoned skin off a dozen roast chickens, a Scotch egg with piccalilli and an excellent trifle are ever-present, but that menu has another candidate with gunpowder potatoes. I'm never too full to eat this: the prospect of the spices dancing on the tongue with the nutty potatoes just refreshes my appetite. The use of the gunpowder spice mix and whole spices works so well here, with the cumin, mustard and fennel seeds adding punctuating intensity to the spicy whole.

Serves 4 normal humans, or 1 of me

1 tbsp sunflower or vegetable oil

1 tsp cumin seeds

1 tsp brown mustard seeds

½ tsp fennel seeds

20g (¾oz) butter

1 small onion, finely chopped

2 garlic cloves, finely chopped

2 green chillies, thinly sliced

800g (1lb 12oz) new potatoes, chopped into bite-sized pieces

1 tbsp tomato purée (paste)

½ tsp salt

300ml (10fl oz) water

1 batch of gunpowder mix (page 66)

Heat the oil in a large frying pan that has a lid and fry the cumin, brown mustard and fennel seeds for a minute or so until the mustard seeds just start to pop and jump around. Add the butter and onion and cook for 10–15 minutes until the onion is soft and beginning to brown. Stir in the garlic and half of the sliced chilli and cook for a minute more.

Stir in the potatoes, tomato purée, salt and water, then cover and cook for 20 minutes, or until the vegetables are tender and the sauce is rich and thick, removing the lid for the last minute if it needs to dry out a little.

Serve topped with the gunpowder mix and the remaining green chilli.

SVANETI POTATOES

Svanuri marili is one of my favourite spice blends. It hails from Svaneti in Georgia, and as widely as I use it, this may be my favourite way.

Serves 4

1kg (2lb 4oz) floury potatoes, cut into 2cm (¾in) dice (I leave the skin on)

½ batch of svanuri marili (page 71)

Oil, for deep-frying

Put the diced potatoes in a pan and rinse until the water runs clear, then fill with clean water. Bring to the boil, spooning away any foam rising to the surface, then lower the heat to a simmer and cook for 3 minutes. Turn off the heat and use a slotted spoon to lift the potatoes into a colander, then on to a large flat tray in a single layer to cool completely, while also drying out.

Fill a deep-fat fryer or a large pan (no more than one-third full) with oil and heat to 110°C/230°F for the first fry. Place a large flat dish beside the fryer, lined with baking parchment. Cook the potatoes in batches until pale and tender. Lift from the oil with a slotted spoon, shaking to drip as much oil into the pan as possible, and lay on the paper in a single layer.

Increase the temperature to 180°C/350°F and fry the potatoes again until very crisp and golden. Use the slotted spoon to lift them from the oil to the baking parchment, then on to a platter. Immediately cast the svanuri marili over and toss to mix. Serve with something very cold to drink.

CHIMICHURRI NEW POTATOES

As spring thinks about summer and the first potatoes of the season are lifted, I usually reach for a few handfuls of sorrel and a little butter to cast into the pan, to dissolve and make its own sauce; this year, chimichurri won. This South American sauce – classically a partner for steak – brings a fine balance of grassy herbs and spicy depth in sharp oily form, and I like it every bit as much here as I do with a medium-rare.

Serves 4

1kg (2lb 4oz) new potatoes

2–3 tbsp chimichurri (page 62)

good pinch or 2 of salt

Boil the potatoes until just cooked – this can be as quick as 8 minutes for small, fresh new potatoes. Drain and allow to release a little heat for a minute.

Tip the potatoes back into the pan, add the chimichurri, replace the lid and swirl the pan around to coat the potatoes. Taste and adjust the salt if necessary, then serve immediately.

CHAAT SWEET POTATOES

Chaat masala's aromatic sourness works beautifully with so many ingredients, it's easy to find yourself sprinkling it over chips, on eggs, into a pan of softening aubergines, across roasted cauliflower … this is my current favourite place for it. Great as a side to roast vegetables or meat of most kinds.

Serves 4

4 large sweet potatoes, scrubbed and each cut into 6 wedges

good drizzle of olive oil

½ batch of chaat masala (page 62), plus extra to serve

1 bunch of spring onions (scallions), thinly sliced with just a little of the green

1 tsp chilli flakes

handful of Bombay mix, plus extra to serve

handful of fresh coriander (cilantro), roughly chopped

small handful of chives, finely chopped

sea salt and freshly ground black pepper

pomegranate molasses, to finish

yoghurt, to serve (optional)

Preheat the oven to 180°C/350°F/gas mark 4 and line a baking tray with baking parchment.

Place the sweet potato wedges on the lined baking tray and drizzle olive oil over the cut sides. Season well with salt and pepper and dust generously with chaat. Cook in the centre of the oven for 30 minutes until cooked through and colouring a little at the edges.

Transfer to a warm serving plate and scatter with the remaining ingredients, finishing with a generous swashing of pomegranate molasses, a little more chaat, much more Bombay mix and perhaps a little yoghurt.

SOUSED MACKEREL

Every spring when I catch the first hint of summer on the breeze, I know the mackerel are on their way. I resolve to fish more. Standing on the beach doing nothing more than the occasional cast in search of my tea makes me feel right. I'm not so fussed if I get lucky; it's the time, the place and the pursuit that settles my soul. If my luck's in and the line tightens, that mackerel will be cooked on the beach or make the short journey back home for this recipe. Herring might be the traditional fish for sousing – and more appropriate to the Dutch heritage and Scandinavian flavours of this recipe – but I just about prefer it with mackerel, at least if I've caught it myself. This is good and large on the allspice, and all the better for it. You can serve it with whatever you like: a potato salad, heavy on the horseradish, is highly recommended.

Serves 4
800ml (1¾ pints) water
90g (3¼oz) salt
8 fresh mackerel, scaled, gutted and filleted

For the pickle
500ml (1 pint) cider vinegar (or white wine vinegar)
250ml (9fl oz) water
1 large onion, very thinly sliced
2 tsp allspice berries
2 tsp black peppercorns
1 fresh bay leaf
2 tbsp soft light brown sugar
pared zest of 1 orange and 1 lemon, or 2 of either, in strips

First, make a basic brine by heating the water with the salt until the salt is completely dissolved. Allow to cool completely. Add the mackerel to the brine and leave for about 2 hours.

Meanwhile, put all the pickle ingredients into another pan, bring slowly to the boil and simmer for a couple of minutes. Allow to cool completely.

Take the fish fillets from the brine and pat them dry. Lay them flat in a suitable sterilized and non-reactive container (glass, stainless steel or plastic) and pour the pickle over. Cover and place in the fridge for at least 5 days before eating. They're best eaten after 5–10 days, but will keep for up to a month. The longer you leave them the softer they become.

To serve, drain the fillets from the pickle and serve with some of the sliced onion.

MANCHAMANTELES

This incredible mole – a type of Mexican sauce – is so good with pretty much any meat, fish, or vegetable that I present it here in its solo glory so that it's not lost in a wider recipe. Try it with the guajillo grilled courgettes (see page 138) and you'll have found a new friend. Pasilla or ancho chillies are perfect here. And careful, manchamanteles means 'tablecloth stainer', thanks to achiote's deep red colour.

Serves 4

3 ancho chillies (or use pasilla)

1 small onion, quartered

4 garlic cloves, left whole in their skins

2 tomatoes, halved

50ml (2fl oz) olive oil

2 tbsp achiote seeds

½ medium pineapple, cut into bite-sized pieces (or use 200g/7oz ready-prepared)

1 green apple, peeled, cored and roughly chopped

1 tbsp sugar

1 tsp ground cinnamon

small pinch of ground cloves

½ tsp ground allspice

50g (2oz) whole almonds

100ml (3½fl oz) water

2 bay leaves

sea salt and freshly ground black pepper

Break the chillies open and shake out and discard the seeds. In a frying pan over a medium–high heat, dry-fry the chillies for a minute, shaking the pan to turn them over. Put in a bowl, cover with boiling water and leave to soak for 10 minutes.

Add the onion, garlic cloves and tomato halves cut side up to the same dry pan and cook for 10 minutes, or until they're soft and the skins are starting to char here and there.

Heat the oil in a separate frying pan and fry the achiote for a minute until the oil turns red, then remove from the heat. Strain the oil, discarding the achiote seeds, then return the oil to the pan and put to one side.

Discard the skins of the charred onion, garlic and tomatoes. Blend the charred veg with the soaked chillies (discarding the soaking liquid), 1 teaspoon of salt, the pineapple, apple, sugar, ground spices, almonds and water to a smooth sauce.

Fry the sauce in the red oil with the bay leaves for a couple of minutes, then cook over a lowish heat for 20 minutes or so until the sauce is rich and thick with spots of oil on the surface. Season to taste with salt and pepper.

Pictured overleaf.

GUAJILLO GRILLED COURGETTES

Guajillos are gently hot, dried chillies from Mexico, with a thin smooth skin that reminds me visually of semi-dried festive dates. Bright and lively, they are widely available as dried flakes that repay in flavour a few moments warmed in a dry pan.

I first made this in the oven, but under the grill gives you a soft upper and a firmly textured underside to the courgettes, which is so very good. A great side as is, this is just the best with the manchamanteles sauce on page 137. If you have dried Mexican oregano, a little dusting over the top before grilling is a fine idea.

Serves 4

4 courgettes (zucchini), cut in half lengthways

2 tbsp olive oil

2 tsp guajillo chilli flakes

sea salt and freshly ground black pepper

Preheat the grill (broiler) to high.

Score the cut side of the courgettes with a knife and toss in the oil. Season with salt and pepper and place cut side up on a baking tray. Sprinkle with the chilli flakes and grill (broil) for 5–7 minutes until lightly charred but still firm.

SEVEN-SPICE ROAST SPROUTS

As is often the case with me, this is not so much a recipe as a suggestion for approaching something. Roasting is my favourite way with sprouts: they can take the heat of the oven as well as stand up to the heat of spice. This is so good, but it is only a springboard: try this with olio santo and garam masala, la-yu chilli oil and panch phoran, or sesame oil and qalat daqqa in place of the olive oil and seven-spice. A squeeze of lemon or lime juice over, to serve, can be perfect, depending on what you are serving them with.

Serves 4

500g (1lb 2oz) Brussels sprouts

1 tbsp olive oil

a heavy bombardment of shichimi togarashi (page 70)

generous pinch of salt

Preheat the oven to 200°C/400°F/gas mark 6.

Remove any darker and damaged outer leaves from the sprouts and cut them in half. Place in a bowl and toss with the oil. Tip on to a baking tray and shower with shichimi togarashi.

Roast in the oven for 10 minutes. Serve dusted with a generous pinch of sea salt.

PANCH PHORAN ROAST CARROTS WITH RAITA AND PISTACHIOS

This simplest of sides shows panch phoran off beautifully; it's perfect with roast lamb, and/or with roast aubergines and cauliflower. It's a very adaptable recipe: fresh coriander works well and, of course, choose a different chilli pepper if you fancy.

Serves 4

500g (1lb 2oz) small carrots

50ml (2fl oz) extra virgin olive oil

1 tsp sea salt

1 tsp panch phoran (page 68)

mustard seed and mint raita (page 88)

50g (2oz) pistachios, crushed

finely chopped fennel or dill leaves

a good grinding of black pepper

a few good pinches of Aleppo pepper

pomegranate molasses (optional)

Preheat the oven to 190°C/375°F/gas mark 5.

Place the carrots in a large bowl, add the oil, salt and panch phoran and toss to coat thoroughly. Arrange on a roasting tray, place in the oven and roast for 20–25 minutes until cooked and taking a little colour here and there.

While the carrots are cooking, make the raita (page 88).

Spoon the raita on to a serving platter and add the carrots. Scatter with pistachios, the chopped fennel or dill, black pepper and Aleppo pepper. Swizz with pomegranate molasses (if using). Serve immediately.

BIGGER THINGS

CHIPOTLE EGGS IN PURGATORY

Chipotles are moderately lively jalapeños that have been smoke-dried: their scent and flavour is extraordinary, and peculiarly addictive. While commonly used in Mexican recipes, I find myself adding them to ragù, stews and – one chilli autumn morning – the sauce for this smasher of a breakfast. I say breakfast, but it's as good for lunch or an idle tea. One of those simple, brilliant recipes everyone should have up their sleeve when comfort or assistance with a fluorescent hangover is required at short notice. In the spirit of the tomato and vanilla compote (page 87), you could easily add half a vanilla pod to the cooking tomatoes – it really is delicious – but not if this is for hungover breakfast: no one wants vanilla when they are rough as a badger's.

Serves 4

2 tbsp olive oil

400g (14oz) can chopped tomatoes

1 dried chipotle chilli, split and opened

400g (14oz) tomato passata

4 eggs

4 slices of bread

1 garlic clove, halved

handful of coriander (cilantro) or parsley, roughly chopped

good swizzle of olive oil, chilli oil, or olio santo (page 98)

sea salt and freshly ground black pepper

Warm the olive oil in a medium frying pan over a medium heat. Add the canned tomatoes and the chipotle and use the back of a wooden spoon or a fork to encourage the pieces to semi-break down. Once bubbling well for a couple of minutes, stir in the passata and season well. Add a splash of boiling water if it thickens too much.

Crack each egg and carefully tip into the tomato sauce in turn, at the points of a compass. Cover with a lid and allow to cook for 5 minutes.

In the meantime, toast that bread. Rub each piece with the cut garlic clove generously enough to frighten off vampires.

When the eggs are as you'd like them – after 5 minutes they should be white and have a runny yolk – lift each egg out with a large spoon, taking a large divot of spicy sauce with it, and place one on each piece of garlicky toast.

Sprinkle with salt, pepper and chopped herbs, swizzle with oil and tuck in.

BACON AND CARAWAY TART

Caraway is a little harder to get to know than some spices. Its flavour appears a fairly straightforward peppery aniseed at first, but there is a bittersweet nuttiness, a hint of citrus and an appealing piney, resinous edge I like very much. It suits savoury as much as sweet; it loves bacon fat as as much as sugar; and is as at home sprinkled over toffee apples (page 237) as it is in the pastry of this cracking tart. Make the pastry base and sides as thin as possible, leaving no gaps or holes.

Serves 4–6

For the pastry

250g (9oz) plain (all-purpose) flour, plus extra for rolling

pinch of salt

150g (5oz) butter

1 egg, beaten

2 tsp caraway seeds

For the filling

30g (1oz) butter

200g (7oz) smoked streaky bacon, cut into large lardons

1 onion, thinly sliced

2 bay leaves

200ml (7fl oz) double (heavy) cream (or use crème fraîche)

2 eggs

1 tbsp Dijon mustard

small bunch of parsley, finely chopped

12 cherry tomatoes, halved

generous pinch of caraway seeds

sea salt and freshly ground black pepper

Put the flour, salt and butter in a food processor and whizz until the mixture resembles fine breadcrumbs. Add the egg and caraway and pulse until the mixture just comes together. Bring the dough together with your hands and shape into a flat round. Wrap the pastry in clingfilm (plastic wrap) and rest it in the fridge for 30 minutes.

Remove the pastry from the fridge and roll out to a circle about 24cm (9in) in diameter. Place over a 20cm (8in) tart tin and use your fingers to carefully press the pastry over the tin, pushing it up the sides and into the corners.

Line the base with baking parchment and some baking beans or rice. Return to the fridge for another 30 minutes. Preheat the oven to 180°C/350°F/gas mark 4.

Meanwhile, make the filling. Melt the butter in a pan over a medium heat and fry the bacon until lightly golden and its fat has rendered. Use a slotted spoon to transfer the bacon to a plate, keeping the fat in the pan. Add the onion and bay leaves and cook for 10–15 minutes until very soft. Remove from the heat and add the bacon back to the pan.

In a bowl, mix the cream, eggs and mustard together with a little salt and pepper.

Bake the lined tart case for 10 minutes until firm but not coloured, then remove the baking beans and parchment and return to the oven for 12–15 minutes until cooked through and golden.

Distribute the bacon and onion mixture over the tart base and sprinkle over the parsley. Carefully pour the egg and cream mix into the tart case, giving it a gentle shake to distribute evenly. Add the tomatoes to the top of the tart. Sprinkle with coarsely ground black pepper and the caraway seeds.

Put the tart in the hot oven on a middle shelf and bake for 30–35 minutes until the tart filling is set. Remove from the oven and leave to cool in the tin for 5 or so minutes before turning out and cutting into wedges, removing the bay leaves as you serve.

CHICORY, ORANGE, PICKLED BLACKBERRIES, BLUE CHEESE AND WALNUT SALAD WITH CORIANDER AND ANARDANA

I've been making variations on this salad for years. One time I'll be obsessed with grapefruit and labneh, another it might be hazelnuts and capers that I can't be without. Behold, this winter's salad, for when bitter leaves and complementing flavours are what you need. It's pretty good in summer's heat too, to be fair. You can use fresh blackberries instead of pickled, and the Cape Malay spiced nuts (page 104) are so good here instead of straight walnuts. A crucial detail: leaving the coriander coarse gives it bold punctuation in the salad, whereas the anardana powder seasons the whole. Splattering the dressing is important: the spices catch there, accentuating that contrast of mouthfuls of intense flavour and others less so. In something so simple and exposed, quality of ingredient shines through: use really good oranges (blood oranges are a nice), the best coriander seeds, an excellent blue cheese, and so on.

Serves 4

60g (2¼oz) walnuts

1 tsp coriander seeds

1–2 oranges, peeled and each segment sliced from the membranes

4 small-medium chicory, leaves separated

80g (3oz) black olives

100g (3½oz) blue cheese, broken into smallish nuggets

12–16 pickled blackberries (page 84)

small handful of dill, roughly chopped

dill honey mustard dressing (page 180)

1 tsp anardana

Toast the walnuts in a dry frying pan over a moderate heat for a few minutes, agitating the pan frequently to prevent them burning. Break them into pieces and tip them into a bowl. Toast the coriander seeds in the same way and crush them in a mortar and pestle only until they form coarse nuggets rather than too fine.

On a serving platter, lay a base of orange slices and scatter the chicory over. Dot with olives, walnuts and nuggets of cheese. Scatter the dill over and splatter with the dressing. Sprinkle with the coriander seeds and anardana and serve.

ZA'ATAR FRUIT FATTOUSH

This is such a bright, refreshing fruit variation of this classic Middle Eastern salad, with the sour thrill of za'atar in two forms bringing spice and punch. There is much scope for altering the feel of this: honeyed grapes – such as muscats – bring sweet richness; leaving the parsley leaves whole makes a bolder impression than when chopped; and the nature of the bread makes such a difference. By all means tweak as you like or to what you have in the fridge. Depending on your need for authenticity, you can make these with bought pitta breads, parathas (page 107) or even himbasha (page 108).

Serves 4

2 flatbreads

½ batch of za'atar vinaigrette (page 101)

2 tbsp natural yoghurt

200g (7oz) watermelon, peeled, deseeded and cubed

2 apples, cored and thinly sliced

100g (3½oz) cherries, halved and stoned

100g (3½oz) white grapes, halved

1 romaine lettuce, shredded

½ cucumber, peeled, deseeded and thinly sliced

½ red onion, very thinly sliced

big bunch of parsley (leaves only)

1cm (½in) thick ponytail of chives, roughly chopped

1 tbsp za'atar (page 72)

Toast the flatbreads (or cook in a low oven) until they are crisp and dry. Allow them to cool then break them into pieces.

In a large bowl, stir the vinaigrette and yoghurt together until well combined. Add the fruit, vegetables and bread and toss gently but thoroughly. Arrange on a platter, scatter with the herbs and za'atar.

CHORIZO

When we kept pigs, I used to make salami and chorizo every autumn. It became part of the bounce of the year. I loved the wait while the cold winter breeze slowly drove the moisture from the charcuterie until it was hard as a hammer and ready to eat, around the time piglets arrived the following year. Without the pigs' presence, the wait no longer forms part of the circle – it no longer makes sense – and I find myself making this cooking chorizo instead. It may not be traditional, but it has the flavours of its Iberian heritage, there's no wait until you can use it, and it is so good. It's quick, simple, delicious and makes incredible patties, burgers, meatballs, mince for ragù, and an exceptional scotching coat for an egg (page 154).

Makes 800g (1lb 12oz)

800g (1lb 12oz) pork mince

2 tbsp smoked hot paprika

2 tbsp sweet paprika

2 tbsp cayenne or Aleppo pepper

4 tbsp fennel seeds

3 garlic cloves, finely chopped

good pinch of salt

about 4 tbsp red wine

Using your hands, mix everything but the wine thoroughly together in a large bowl. Add enough wine to bring everything together and incorporate well. Keep in the fridge and use within a couple of days.

MERGUEZ

The classic merguez sausage hails from the North African countries bordering the Mediterranean. It makes me very happy. I've taken the spirit of it and the spices that give it its characteristic warm, arresting embrace to make this mix for cooking into burgers, meatballs and so on, in much the same way as I'd use the chorizo above. It also makes an excellent Scotch egg (page 154).

Makes 800g (1lb 12oz)

800g (1lb 12oz) lamb mince

3 tbsp harissa (page 66)

2 tbsp fennel seeds, toasted and lightly crushed

1 tbsp smoked hot paprika

2 tsp unsmoked sweet paprika

generous pinch of ground cinnamon

2 tsp salt

1 tsp celery seeds

2 tsp dried mint

Using your hands, mix everything thoroughly together in a large bowl. Keep in the fridge and use within a couple of days.

SPICY SCOTCH EGGS

A Scotch egg might be my favourite of what Bob Mortimer calls 'pocket meats'. Given its competition from the sausage roll, pasty, salami etc., that's quite the compliment. I am never not hungry for a Scotch egg: if one is in the house, it calls my name in the same way a Toblerone, trifle or the last Magnum in the freezer does.

If you are cooking these to be eaten at the same time and you want them warm, you might want to preheat the oven to 140°C/280°F/gas mark 1 to keep the earlier eggs warm while the rest cook. Bear in mind that the first egg cooks quickest as the oil is hottest; allow a little time for it to get back up to temperature between eggs if you can.

Makes 6

7–8 eggs

60g (2¼oz) plain (all-purpose) flour

75g (2½oz) panko breadcrumbs

1 batch of either merguez or chorizo (page 153), cold from the fridge

1–2 litres (2–4 pints) sunflower oil

Place 6 of the eggs in a large pan of cold water and bring to the boil. Reduce the heat and simmer for 4 minutes. Place under cold running water for a few minutes until cool. Peel carefully and set aside.

Place the flour and breadcrumbs in separate bowls and beat the remaining egg(s) in another.

Gently roll each egg in the flour and brush off any excess.

Divide the spicy meat into six and form each into a flat circular burger a little less than 5–7mm (¼in) thick. Carefully shape the meat patty evenly around each egg, using gentle pressure to seal up the joins.

Roll each in flour, brushing off any excess. Then roll each in the beaten egg, allowing the excess to drip off before rolling in the breadcrumbs, turning the eggs to coat them evenly. Place them on a plate and into the fridge.

Pour the oil into a pan so that it comes around 6cm (2½in) up the side. Heat the oil to 170°C/340°F. Fry – in batches to suit the pan size and to avoid the oil being more than two-thirds up the side – until the breadcrumbs are golden. Remove using a slotted spoon and drain on kitchen paper. Piccalilli (page 83) and/or kimchi mayo (simply blend a generous spoon of kimchi with four times as much mayonnaise) are compulsory to go with.

HARIRA SOUP

One day I shall write a book of soups, and within it shall be a chapter dedicated to main course soups, and within that shall be a version of this heartening taste of Morocco. The spicy heat of harissa, the sweetness of cinnamon and ginger and the soft bitterness of turmeric come together to such great effect. I make endless versions of this that reflect what I have in the house: leftover roasted vegetables instead of the chicken, vermicelli instead of orzo, and a handful of chopped kale might make an appearance now and again. It is highly adaptable and often gets further from its authentic Moroccan origins, but the spicing reminds me of where I owe the pleasure it gives.

Serves 4

2 tbsp olive oil

1 large onion, finely diced

2 tsp ground ginger

2 tsp ground coriander

10cm (4in) cinnamon stick

1 tsp ground turmeric

3 tbsp concentrated tomato purée (paste)

2 x 400g (14oz) cans chopped tomatoes

1 litre (2 pints) water

180g (6oz) puy lentils, rinsed

2 carrots, grated

100g (3½oz) orzo pasta

400g (14oz) leftover cooked chicken, chopped

4 tsp harissa (page 66)

good handful of coriander (cilantro), roughly chopped

sea salt and freshly ground black pepper

In a large heavy-based pan, warm the oil over a low–medium heat and cook the onion slowly until soft and translucent, stirring often: this is likely to be 15 minutes minimum. Season generously.

Add the spices and cook for a minute. Stir in the tomato purée, the chopped tomatoes and the water. Bring to a simmer and add the lentils, turning the heat to low. Cook for 15 minutes, then add the grated carrot. Stir occasionally and add a little water if needed. Season.

Once the lentils are cooked, add the orzo and chicken. Simmer until the orzo is cooked – this will vary depending on the type chosen. Taste and season as required.

Ladle into bowls – it should be on the thicker side of thin – swirl harissa on the surface of each and sprinkle with coriander.

PARADISE CAULIFLOWER SOUP

I usually roast cauliflower if I'm using it in a soup, but here I prefer its clean unroasted flavour against the peanut butter and the spices. The nuttiness of the spices chats to the peanut butter, which just sits at the back where you want it. Serve with flatbreads or sourdough.

Serves 4

2 tsp coriander seeds

2 tsp grains of paradise

1 tbsp butter

1 tbsp olive oil

1 onion, finely chopped

2 garlic cloves

2 tsp sugar

1 medium/large cauliflower, chopped into 3–4cm (1–1½in) cubes

1.2 litres (2½ pints) hot chicken or vegetable stock

6 tbsp peanut butter

small bunch of parsley, finely chopped

sea salt and freshly ground black pepper

Toast the coriander seeds and grains of paradise in a dry pan over a medium heat until they become fragrant, agitating the pan to prevent burning. Reduce to a moderately coarse powder using a mortar and pestle or spice grinder.

Warm the butter and oil in a large pan over a medium heat. Reduce the heat and add the onion and a pinch of salt. Cook, stirring frequently, for 15 minutes or so until translucent and soft. Add the garlic, sugar and half the spice mix and stir well.

Add the cauliflower and the stock and bring to the boil. Reduce the heat and simmer for 12–15 minutes until the cauliflower is cooked but firm. Remove from the heat and, once a little cooler, pour half into a blender along with half the peanut butter. Blend until smoothish. Decant into another container, then blend the remaining soup and peanut butter.

Warm the soup through before serving, seasoning to taste with salt and pepper. Sprinkle with the rest of the spice mix and the chopped parsley.

SPICY RAMEN by Yuki Gomi

Some time ago, I spent a morning in the virtual company of Yuki Gomi. Under her charming expert instruction I made miso, or rather I made what after a year or so of fermentation would become miso. Now that time has elapsed, I can tell you it is quite extraordinary. Not content with stealing her expertise, I twisted her arm for this recipe: it is such a special ramen, and far simpler in practice than its numerous steps imply.

Serves 2

For the dashi (or omit and simply use chicken stock)

1 or 2 pieces of dried kombu (around 5cm/2in square)

4 dried shiitake mushrooms

700ml (1 ½ pints) water

For the ten men jyan sauce

3 tbsp red or dark miso

2 tsp dark brown sugar

1 tbsp oriental mushroom sauce or kecap manis (page 94)

1 tsp soy sauce

For the cauliflower miso

100g (3 ½ oz) super-firm tofu

½ cauliflower (around 300g/10oz)

4 shiitake mushrooms (use the mushrooms soaked to make the dashi, or use fresh ones)

1 tbsp vegetable oil

3cm (1in) fresh ginger, finely chopped

1 garlic clove, finely chopped

2 tbsp ten men jyan sauce (see above)

1–2 tsp shichimi togarashi (page 70)

Start by making the dashi broth. Wipe the kombu with a clean cloth. Rinse the shiitakes. Put the water in a deep pan and soak both for at least 30 minutes (and up to 2 days in advance for a more developed flavour) in the fridge.

Squeeze out the mushrooms and set them to one side for the cauliflower miso. Leave the kombu in the water and heat up slowly; just as the water comes to a boil, remove from the heat and take out the kombu. You can eat the kombu at this stage, if you like; it is super nutritious. The dashi is now ready: set it to one side.

Now make the ten men jyan sauce by simply mixing all the ingredients together. Set aside.

To make the cauliflower miso, start by squeezing out the excess water in the tofu by hand over a sink. You can then break up the tofu by hand, or chop finely with a knife. Separately, chop the cauliflower very finely with a knife or grate with a cheese grater or food processor. Finely chop 2 of the shiitake mushrooms.

Heat the vegetable oil in a pan and sauté the cauliflower, chopped shiitake mushroom, ginger and garlic for a few minutes. Next, add the tofu and cook for another few minutes, then reduce the heat and add 2 tablespoons of the ten men jyan sauce and the shichimi togarashi. Mix well and place to one side.

Quickly blanch the green vegetables, ready for topping the ramen, and set to one side.

Continued overleaf

For the ramen broth

any green vegetables: baby spinach, pak choi or kale etc.

150–200g (5–7oz) ramen noodles/egg noodles

700ml (1½ pints) dashi (see previous page) or chicken stock

½ tbsp sake (optional)

2 tsp mirin

2–3 tbsp light tahini

2 tbsp soy sauce

1 tbsp red miso

2 tbsp la-yu chilli oil (see below), plus extra (optional) to serve

3 spring onions (scallions)

fried onions, to serve

In a separate pan filled with boiling water, add the noodles and cook for 1–2 minutes. The exact time depends on which noodles you have. Please check the instructions on the package.

To make the ramen broth, reheat the dashi by bringing it to the boil in a large pan. Add the sake (if using), mirin, tahini, soy sauce, miso and la-yu chilli oil. Pour the hot ramen broth into each bowl and add a portion of the strained noodles. Then add a generous helping of the cauliflower miso. Finish with the green vegetable toppings, spring onions, fried onions and a little extra chilli oil, if you like. Serve immediately, or the noodles will become soggy.

LA-YU CHILLI OIL by Yuki Gomi

One taste of this sesame chilli oil and you'll be using it on noodles, in dressings, and most definitely in the ramen recipe above. This is best made as a cold infusion, left for a few days for the flavours to develop, but if you just can't wait or are short on time, gently heat up the oil and spices, to infuse them, then use immediately once cool.

Makes 100ml (3½fl oz)

1 tbsp shichimi togarashi (page 70)

100ml (3½fl oz) sunflower or rapeseed oil

2 tsp toasted sesame oil

Add all the ingredients to a bottle or jar and leave them to infuse for a few days.

SAFFRON RICE

This wonderful Persian rice (aka tahdig) is a little git to get just right – i.e. so it leaves the pan with perfect crust intact – but it tastes so good that even the imperfect attempts are deeply worthwhile. A friend's dad gave him two bits of golfing advice when he started playing: keep your head still, and keep your fucking head still. The spirit of that advice applies to lifting the lid up part way through the cooking: don't. Keep the heat low, have faith and test it for doneness only near the end.

This may seem suspiciously simple in terms of ingredients, but therein lies its charm: the barberries bring sour punctuation, saffron the inky gentle bitterness, and that light and shade between crust and the softer body within is beyond special. If you find yourself spooning some of that crust out of the pan and on to the turned-out rice, you won't be the only one. This really is superb with a stew.

Serves 4

big pinch of saffron

300g (10oz) basmati rice

30g (1oz) butter

handful of dried barberries

sea salt and freshly ground black pepper

Bring a large pan of salted water to the boil.

Soak the saffron in 2 tablespoons of the freshly boiled water.

Add the rice to the salted water and simmer for 6 minutes until the ends of the grains of rice are just cooked with the centres still crunchy. Drain well.

Melt the butter in a large frying pan over a medium heat, then add the par-cooked rice and an enthusiastic grind of pepper and pour over the saffron, including the liquid. Cook over a high heat for a few minutes, or until you can hear the rice sizzling, then turn the heat right down and cover very tightly. Steam gently for 20 minutes or so until you have a golden crust of rice on the bottom of the pan and the rice is cooked through. Put a tea towel under the lid and rest for 5 minutes

Turn out on to a plate with the crispy rice from the bottom of the pan on the top of the softer rice. Sprinkle with the barberries and serve.

BOURRIDE

Whether you get the fish from a supermarket or fishmonger, ask them to fillet the fish and give you the bones too, to make the broth: it makes for a finer bourride. If you have fillets only, simply use a litre of fish stock instead of water. A confetti of finely chopped parsley, tarragon or chervil – whichever suits the weather – is the perfect final flourish.

Serves 4

1 tbsp olive oil

2 celery sticks, thinly sliced

2 leeks, white parts only, thinly sliced

2 onions, thinly sliced

2 garlic cloves, finely chopped

2 tsp fennel seeds, lightly crushed

big pinch of chilli flakes, or more to taste

a strip of orange peel

1 bay leaf

2 tbsp tomato purée (paste)

500g (1lb 2oz) fish bones (or 1 litre/2 pints fish stock, see intro)

1 glass of dry white wine

800g–1kg (1lb 12oz–2lb 4oz) mixed fish fillets/shellfish

big pinch of saffron

200g (7oz) aioli (page 97), plus extra to serve

small bunch of herbs, finely chopped

sea salt and freshly ground black pepper

toasted sourdough, to serve

Heat the oil in a large pan over a medium heat, add the vegetables and garlic and cook for about 15 minutes, stirring frequently, until soft. Add the spices, orange peel, bay leaf, tomato purée and fish bones and cook for a few minutes. Add the wine and simmer until reduced by half. Add 1 litre (1¾ pints) water (or fish stock if not using bones) and bring to the boil. Simmer for 10–15 minutes until the broth is slightly reduced.

Strain the broth through a sieve, squeezing out as much liquid as possible. Heat the broth over a medium heat and season to taste with salt and pepper. Add the fish/shellfish and saffron and gently cook until the fish is just cooked and firm. Use a slotted spoon to remove the fish and share it equally between four bowls.

Whisk 150ml (5fl oz) of the broth into the aioli, then whisk back into the pan and cook for a few minutes without boiling until slightly thickened. Ladle over the fish in each bowl, sprinkle with herbs, and serve with toasted bread and more aioli.

MOUCLADE

I first ate this years ago on the Charente-Maritime coast of western France. A few days exploring where land meets the sea for its food and for the potential to relocate proved rewarding in the former and less so in the latter, but a sunny tipsy lunch of mussels was most welcome. I was surprised to find curry powder paired with mussels, especially in France, but it is something of a classic of this coast, likely as a result of La Rochelle's port trade with the East. The character of the curry powder is all-important: it should be mild, and while shop-bought will be fine, making the blend on page 70 will reward your trouble.

Serves 4

1.5kg (3lb 5oz) mussels, cleaned

100ml (3½fl oz) dry white wine

25g (1oz) butter

1 small onion, finely chopped

1 leek, trimmed and thinly sliced

2 garlic cloves, finely chopped

2 tsp mild curry powder

2 tbsp cognac

2 tsp plain (all-purpose) flour

200g (7oz) crème fraîche

small bunch of parsley, finely chopped

sea salt and freshly ground black pepper

Put the mussels and wine in a large pan, cover and cook over a high heat for 3–4 minutes, shaking the pan now and then, until the mussels have opened.

Drain the mussels in a colander set over a bowl to catch the cooking liquor. Put the mussels in a large serving bowl and cover to keep warm.

Melt the butter in a pan, add the onion, leek, garlic and curry powder and cook gently, without browning, for a few minutes. Add the cognac and cook until it has almost evaporated, then stir in the flour and cook for another minute. Gradually stir in all but the last tablespoon or so of the mussel liquor. Bring the sauce to a simmer and cook for 2–3 minutes.

Add the crème fraîche and simmer for another minute or so, stirring to combine. Season, stir in the parsley and pour the sauce over the mussels, retaining the last little bit where any grit might be sitting. Serve with excellent bread, a white wine that's drier than a monkey's paw, and eat in the sun.

MAPO TOFU by Li Ling Wang

This is one of the great recipes of Sichuan province, China. Central to its excellence is the notion of 'ma la': the numbing pungency (ma) that sets the tongue and lips tingling, and spicy heat (la) from the pepper and the chillies. The numbing ma allows you to take more fiery la. This distinction and the balance between the two is central to that region's cooking, and Sichuan pepper is the key. Mapo tofu shows that off perfectly. It might seem peculiar to pair tofu with pork, but it works so well. I am indebted to Li Ling Wang – friend and collaborator Matt Williamson's mother-in-law – for such a glorious recipe.

Serves 4

350g (12oz) firm tofu, cut into bite-sized pieces

2 tbsp sesame seeds

1½ tbsp chilli flakes

2 tsp ground Sichuan pepper

80ml (3fl oz) sunflower or vegetable oil

1 tbsp finely grated fresh ginger, plus 1 slice fresh ginger

big bunch of spring onions (scallions), white and green separated and thinly sliced

2 tbsp sesame oil

4 garlic cloves, finely chopped

120g (4oz) pork mince

1 tbsp cornflour (cornstarch)

150ml (5fl oz) water

2 tbsp soy sauce

1 tsp sugar

sea salt

Place the tofu into a bowl and cover with freshly boiled water. Soak for 10 minutes, then drain well. Put the sesame seeds in a small heatproof bowl with half the chilli flakes and 1 teaspoon of the Sichuan pepper. Heat the sunflower or vegetable oil with the slice of ginger until it just begins to sizzle. Pour it over the sesame seed mix and put to one side.

Fry the white part of the spring onions with the garlic and grated ginger in sesame oil for 1 minute until just soft, then add the pork mince and cook for 5–7 minutes until just beginning to colour.

Mix the cornflour with the water and soy sauce, then add this to the pan along with the sugar, and salt to taste. Bring to the boil and then add the tofu and simmer gently for 5 minutes. Discard the ginger slice from the chilli oil and stir through the tofu to taste (with all the sesame and spices) along with the spring onion greens. Add salt to taste.

Serve with plain rice, something sharp like pickled radishes, steamed vegetables and the remaining chilli flakes and Sichuan chilli on the side to sprinkle over the top.

BÚN RIÊU

This Vietnamese classic is a bowl of pleasure: fresh and sour from the lime, yet full of comfort. There are many variations on this theme but I love the combination of the meatballs, tomato and crab. While neither is strictly essential, two seemingly small details make a difference: the oil made with achiote adds its characteristic flavour and colour, and white pepper (if at all possible, from the Vietnamese island of Phu Quoc) brings a special heat and fragrance. That said, it's mighty fine with a good black pepper too.

Serves 4

150g (5oz) pork mince or skinned sausage

150g (5oz) peeled raw prawns (shrimp), finely chopped

3 tsp fish sauce

1 tsp cracked white pepper

4 garlic cloves, finely chopped

2 tbsp finely grated fresh ginger

1 tsp sugar

pinch of sea salt

2 shallots, or 1 small onion, roughly chopped

2 lemongrass stalks, thinly sliced

2 tsp chilli flakes

5 tbsp olive oil

4 tomatoes, finely chopped

1 litre (2 pints) chicken stock

3 tsp achiote seeds

200g (7oz) dried vermicelli rice noodles

200g (7oz) crabmeat

2 juicy limes

150g (5oz) beansprouts

½ bunch of spring onions (scallions), thinly sliced

small bunch of mint and/or coriander (cilantro), leaves picked

Using a food processor, blend the pork mince with the prawns, 1 teaspoon of the fish sauce, half the pepper, half the garlic, half the ginger, the sugar and salt to a smoothish mix, adding a tiny splash of water if necessary. Place in the fridge until ready to use.

Next, blend the shallot with the lemongrass, 1 teaspoon of fish sauce, half of the chilli flakes, and the rest of pepper, ginger and garlic to a fairly smooth paste, adding a splash of water if necessary.

Heat 1 tablespoon of the oil in a frying pan over a medium heat and fry the shallot and lemongrass paste with half the tomatoes for 10 minutes or so until the tomatoes have broken down. Add the chicken stock, cover and simmer for 30 minutes.

Heat the remaining 4 tablespoons of oil in a small frying pan over a medium heat and fry the achiote seeds and remaining chilli flakes for a minute or so until the seeds just start to sizzle and release their colour. Immediately remove from the heat and leave to infuse.

Soak or cook the noodles following the packet instructions, then strain and divide between four warm bowls.

Drop heaped tablespoons of the pork and prawn mix into the broth, then add the crabmeat, the remaining teaspoon of fish sauce and the remaining tomatoes. Bring it back to the boil and simmer for 5 minutes or so until the meatballs are cooked through. Remove from the heat. Strain the achiote oil (discarding the seeds) and add to the broth.

Stir the juice of one of the limes into the broth, then ladle it over the noodles in each bowl. Add beansprouts, spring onions and the mint/coriander to each. Serve with the remaining lime cut into wedges. A scant dash of sriracha (page 89) is ideal if you fancy a livener.

SAMBAL GORENG TEMPE by Lara Lee

Sambal goreng, which translates as 'fried sambal' in Indonesian, is a whole class of dishes where sambal – the chilli condiment eaten all over Indonesia (of which there are hundreds of variations) – is transformed into a spice paste (bumbu) when it's fried in hot oil. This version is my go-to, a caramelized sambal goreng with tempe (spelled 'tempeh' in English) that's fried until crunchy, nutty and irresistibly toasty. Think of this as your new favourite 'whatever's in the pantry' recipe: swap the vegetables and sub the tempe for another protein like diced chicken, slivers of pork or beef, or cubes of firm tofu. The heart of a good sambal goreng is the sambal itself, and this version is fragrant with ginger, garlic and shallots, the tang of tamarind and the defining warmth of chillies.

Serves 4

350ml (12fl oz) rapeseed oil, plus 4 tbsp

400g (14oz) tempeh, cut into chips

6 medium shallots, chopped

25g (1oz) fresh ginger, peeled and sliced

6 garlic cloves, thinly sliced

2 tomatoes, cut into wedges

2½ tsp tamarind paste

1 tbsp palm or brown sugar

3 tbsp kecap manis (page 94)

200ml (7fl oz) water

2 lemongrass stalks, bruised with a rolling pin

4 makrut lime leaves, torn (optional)

4–6 red serrano or Fresno chillies, deseeded and thinly sliced

2 tsp ground coriander

100g (3½oz) salted roasted peanuts

100g (3½oz) green beans, chopped into 2.5cm (1in) pieces

175g (6oz) lacinato or curly kale, leaves only, chopped

sea salt

Pour the oil into a heavy-based, deep-sided pan, ensuring it is no more than one-third full. Line a baking tray with several sheets of kitchen paper. Heat the oil to 175°C/350°F. If you don't have a kitchen thermometer, check the oil is hot enough by adding a cube of bread; it should turn golden in 15–20 seconds.

Carefully add the first batch of tempeh to the hot oil and fry until golden and crunchy, around 7–9 minutes. When the temperature of the oil returns to 175°C/350°F, fry the second batch. Remove from the oil using a slotted spoon or tongs, and drain on the lined baking tray. Season with a good pinch of salt.

Place the shallots, ginger, garlic, tomatoes and ½ teaspoon of fine salt in the bowl of a food processor and blend to a coarse paste.

Combine the tamarind paste, sugar, kecap manis and water in a jug and set aside.

Heat the 4 tablespoons of oil in a large frying pan or wok over a medium heat. Add the spice paste, lemongrass and lime leaves (if using). Cook for 8 minutes, stirring occasionally, until the paste is fragrant and has started to caramelize. Add the chillies and ground coriander and cook for another 5 minutes, stirring occasionally, until the chillies have softened.

Add the sauce to the pan, along with the peanuts, beans, lacinato or kale, tempeh and a pinch of salt. Cook for 5 minutes or so until the sauce clings to everything and the liquid has evaporated. Serve immediately with steamed white rice.

Note: You can sub kecap manis with a mix of 3 tablespoons of dark soy sauce mixed with 3 tablespoons of brown sugar; instead of the tamarind paste, you can mix 2½ teaspoons of lime juice with 2½ teaspoons of brown sugar. For those less keen on deep-frying, you can pan-fry the tempeh. Heat 4 tablespoons of oil in a frying pan over a high heat and fry the tempe in a single layer (in batches), about 3 minutes on each side. Add more oil as needed.

DOMI-YANGNYEOM-GUI

This quick, delicious and memorable Korean recipe traditionally uses snapper, but bream or sea bass work equally well. As good as the fish may be, the star is the yangnyeomjang sauce, where the salty funk of the soy, the nutty sesame and the squeaky spring onions combine beautifully. The presence of gochugaru flakes – the vivid chilli so characteristic of Korean recipes – is the killer.

Serves 2

2 sustainably farmed whole bream, cleaned

1 tsp fine sea salt

2 tbsp plain (all-purpose) flour

100ml (3½fl oz) vegetable oil

1 batch of yangnyeomjang (page 72)

Sprinkle the fish all over with the salt and place in the fridge for 20 minutes.

Pat the fish dry, then dust with the flour. Heat the oil in a large frying pan over a low heat. Carefully add the fish and cook for about 10 minutes until the underside of the fish turns golden. Turn the fish over and cook for another 10–15 minutes until both sides are well coloured and the fish is cooked through.

Transfer to a plate and spoon the yangnyeomjang sauce over the top.

Pictured opposite.

BLACKENED FISH

This favourite from southern USA gets its name from the delightfully burnt tones the spice mix takes on as it cooks. The flavours are quite full-on and suit a robust fish like salmon or bream, but somewhat peculiarly work with the more delicate trout too. This makes a really gorgeous lunch or quick midweek supper: all it needs are wedges of lemon or lime and a good green salad.

Serves 4

4 x 120g (4oz) trout fillets, skin on

2 tbsp olive oil

1 batch of blackening seasoning (page 61)

40g (1½oz) butter

Pat the trout fillets dry and then coat in 1 tablespoon of the oil. Sprinkle the blackening seasoning over the fillets, fully coating them, and use dry hands to make sure the spices stick to the fish.

Preheat a cast-iron or non-stick frying pan over a medium heat. Add the remaining oil to the pan and, once it is hot, place the fillets flesh side down and cook for 2–3 minutes without moving, to colour and toast the spice coating.

Flip over and cook skin side down for an additional 5–6 minutes, adding the butter after 1 minute and spooning it over and around the fillets as they cook.

Remove from the pan and serve immediately.

VEGETABLE KORMA

It's easy to make a vegetable curry; making a special one is another matter. The secret here is in cooking the vegetables in two groups and in the subtleness of the spicing: taking the flavour of garam masala off to the left with extra green cardamom, there's the soft backdrop of the saffron, and warmth of the cassia.

Serves 4

150g (5oz) baby carrots, peeled

300g (10oz) new potatoes, cut into bite-sized pieces

200g (7oz) cauliflower, cut into bite-sized pieces

300g (10oz) squash, cut into bite-sized pieces

1 tbsp oil

1 tbsp garam masala (page 64)

200g (7oz) green beans, trimmed and halved

200g (7oz) mangetout, halved

100g (3½oz) asparagus, trimmed and cut into 4cm (1½in) pieces

150g (5oz) peas

30g (1oz) butter or ghee

1 onion, thinly sliced

40g (1½oz) cashews, ground to a coarse powder (or use ground almonds)

juice of ½ lemon

100g (3½oz) natural yoghurt

1 tsp sugar

1 cassia stick

8 green cardamom pods

2 bay leaves

1 blade of mace

1 dried Kashmiri chilli (optional)

2 garlic cloves, finely chopped

1 tbsp grated fresh ginger

big pinch of saffron, soaked in 2 tbsp warm water

seeds from 1 pomegranate

small bunch of coriander (cilantro), finely chopped

sea salt and freshly ground black pepper

Preheat the oven to 200°C/400°F/gas mark 6.

In a large bowl, toss the carrots, potatoes, cauliflower and squash with the oil, 1 teaspoon of the garam masala and a big pinch of salt. Tip into a roasting tray and roast for 15–20 minutes until tender. Put to one side.

Bring a big pan of salted water to the boil and cook the green vegetables for 4–5 minutes until tender, then drain and plunge into cold water to stop the cooking. Put to one side.

Melt half the butter or ghee in a pan, add the onion and cook for 10–15 minutes until soft and beginning to turn golden. Transfer to a blender or food processor and blend to a smooth paste with the ground nuts, another teaspoon of the garam masala, the lemon juice, yoghurt and sugar.

In the same pan, fry the whole spices in the remaining butter for 1 minute until fragrant, then add the garlic and ginger and fry for a few seconds. Add the onion paste along with the saffron and its soaking water to the pan and stir for 5 minutes to thicken.

Add 300ml (10fl oz) water and a bit more salt to taste if needed, then cover and gently simmer for about 5 minutes, or until the sauce is rich and thick.

Add the vegetables and warm through, adding a splash of water if you want. Check the seasoning, adding salt, pepper and a squeeze more lemon juice if needed.

Serve sprinkled with the pomegranate seeds, the rest of the garam masala and the coriander. Serve with rice, naan breads or parathas (page 107).

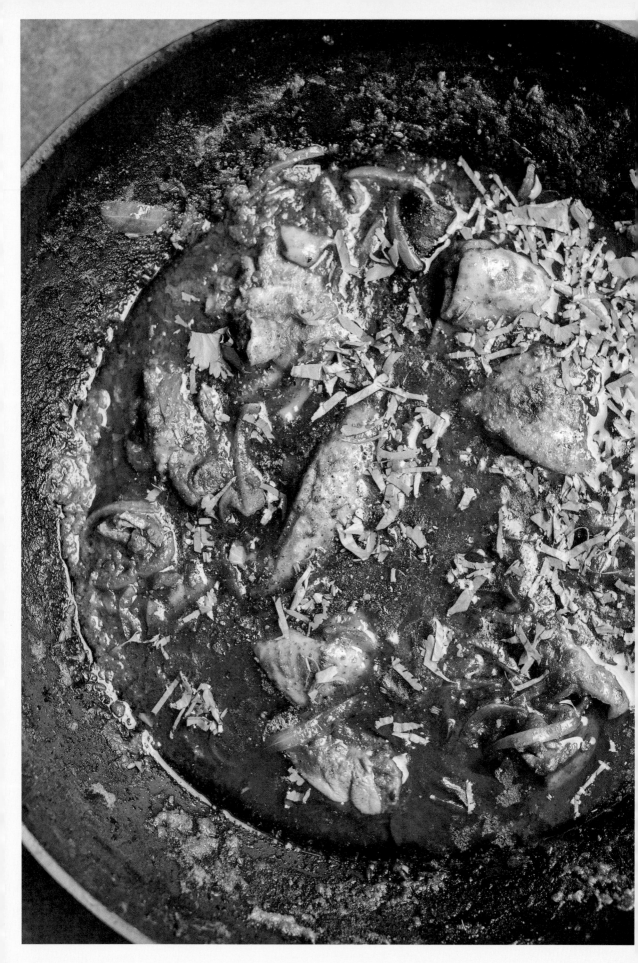

PUNJABI CHICKEN CURRY by Maunika Gowardhan

A classic chicken curry hailing from North India. There are so many memories of eating this on a Sunday afternoon at my home when I lived in India. A plateful of chicken curry and plain rice has always been a family favourite so I am sharing a recipe that has been cooked for years in our home. Using whole spices at the start of cooking is key to bringing an aromatic flavour. Tempered in warm oil, the spices release their flavour and continue to simmer as the curry cooks. For most of my recipes I use cassia bark, a spice that is generally ideal for stewing or braising recipes. It lends a strong, smoky flavour and holds its shape while infusing the gravy. Green cardamom (also known as 'choti elaichi') is added to this recipe whole with the seeds encased for a mellow warmth. Discard the whole spices once the curry is cooked and you are ready to serve.

Serves 4

1½ tsp cumin seeds

4 tbsp ghee or vegetable oil

5cm (2in) cassia bark (or use cinnamon stick if you prefer)

8 green cardamom pods

2 medium white onions, thinly sliced

7 garlic cloves, finely chopped

5cm (2in) fresh ginger, peeled and finely chopped

1½ tsp ground turmeric

1 tsp mild chilli powder

350g (12oz) tomatoes, blended to a purée

700g (1½lb) chicken on the bone, cut into medium pieces (you can use drumstick and thighs)

300ml (10fl oz) chicken stock or water

1 tsp garam masala (page 64)

2 tbsp chopped coriander (cilantro) leaves

sea salt

Coarsely grind the cumin seeds in a pestle and mortar and set aside. Heat the ghee or oil in a large, heavy-based pan over a medium heat. Add ½ teaspoon of the ground cumin seeds, the cassia bark (or cinnamon stick) and green cardamom pods. As they begin to sizzle in the pan, add the onions and cook for about 15 minutes. Stir well, making sure they don't stick to the bottom of the pan.

Add the garlic and ginger and fry for 1 minute, then stir in the turmeric and chilli powder, followed by the blended tomatoes. Cook for 5–7 minutes. Now add the chicken pieces and fry for 10 minutes, stirring well so that the masala coats the pieces and they seal evenly.

Add the stock or water, season to taste and simmer over a low heat for 20 minutes with the lid on, stirring halfway through. Remove from the heat and sprinkle over the remaining ground cumin seeds, the garam masala and fresh coriander. Serve with roti or rice.

JERK CHICKEN

When the sun is high, the breeze pleasing and the scent of factor 50 fills the air, there a few things better to eat than this Jamaican classic. The jerk seasoning – hot chillies, sweet spices and resinous thyme – suits chicken so well, and the marinating gives it time to ease into the meat.

Although the instructions below are for the oven, jerk chicken was originally cooked in a pit and hence is a great one for the barbecue – the smoke of the charcoal makes a welcome ingredient. Traditionally served with rice and peas, I confess to finding it very hard to convince myself to make something to go with this: I just want to eat it, undiluted, and sink into its wonderful fragrant, smoky heat.

Serves 4

1 batch of jerk seasoning (page 67)

½ bunch of spring onions (scallions), finely chopped

3 garlic cloves, peeled but left whole

1 Scotch bonnet chilli, deseeded and finely chopped

1 tbsp brown sugar

1 tbsp soy sauce

juice of 1 lime (plus a few lime wedges to serve)

4 chicken legs

hot sauce, to serve

Blend all of the ingredients (apart from the chicken and hot sauce) to a coarse paste. Rub the marinade paste over the meat and leave to marinate in the fridge for at least an hour – anything up to 24 hours is fine.

Preheat the oven to 200°C/400°F/gas mark 6.

Wrap the chicken in foil and place on a baking tray in the centre of the oven. Cook for 25–35 minutes, or until cooked through to the bone. Remove the foil and cook for a further 2–5 minutes on each side, basting with hot sauce if you want an extra kick. Make sure the chicken is fully cooked through and nicely charred.

Serve with rice. Or not.

NANJING SALTED DUCK

Nanjing is the capital of Jiangsu province, and part of the broad region that falls under Huaiyang cuisine, one of the four great traditions in Chinese cooking. Folklore has it that an emperor of the Ming Dynasty became so disgruntled at the squawks of Nanjing's chickens keeping him awake that he ordered their slaughter, and ducks took their place. Nanjing is now famous for its duck, and salted duck is perhaps its most famous dish, and understandably so. However inauthentic it may sound, I love this with stir-fried greens or a leafy salad, depending on the time of year.

Serves 4–6

1 x 2kg (4lb 8oz) duck, spatchcocked

2 tbsp sea salt

1 tsp freshly ground black pepper

1.5 litres (3 pints) water

4 slices of fresh ginger

½ bunch of spring onions (scallions), thinly sliced

2 bay leaves

3 whole star anise

¼ cinnamon stick

10 black peppercorns

2 tbsp Shaoxing wine (or use dry sherry)

1 tbsp soy sauce

2 tsp zhenjiang vinegar (or use red wine vinegar)

Sprinkle the duck all over with 1 tablespoon of the salt and the ground black pepper, rubbing into the skin, then leave in the fridge, uncovered, for 1–4 hours.

Rinse off the salt and pat dry with a clean tea towel.

Pour the water into a wok or pan large enough to be no more than about 40% full. Add the remaining salt, ginger, spring onion, bay leaves, whole spices, wine, soy sauce and vinegar. Bring to the boil, then reduce to a simmer.

Carefully lower the duck in, breast side up. Cover and cook for 45–60 minutes until tender. Lift out and allow to rest for 5 minutes before chopping or carving into slices.

PAN-FRIED CHICKEN WITH PIMENTÓN DE LA VERA AND MASHED POTATOES by José Pizarro

My oldest friend used to copy my essays in sixth form. He may as well have selected random words from random fairy tales for all the good it did him. We drifted through a few idle post-school years before heading in different directions to – somehow, and without planning – separately arrive in the food world. He has a restaurant in Bermondsey, a hop and a skip from José, the tapas bar. I can think of few places I'd rather be on sunny day than José, eating yet another plate of patatas bravas, marvelling at the joy of sherry and watching the world go by while talking nonsense with my friend.

I'm thrilled José has shared this delicious recipe with us, showing off the unique qualities of pimentón de la Vera perfectly. This is a great example of what can happen when the Venn diagram of people, plants and place come together to beautiful culinary effect. Chilli peppers, originally brought to Spain from Mexico, have been grown in the fertile soils of the la Vera river valley for most of 500 years; once harvested, they are oak-smoked, before being slow-milled (to avoid flavour-changing heat) to a powder. Each increment of experience and terroir sing in the hot, smoked flavour of this special pimentón.

Serves 4

3 tbsp extra virgin olive oil

4 garlic cloves (skin on)

1 bay leaf

8 boneless chicken thighs, halved

1 tsp pimentón de la Vera picante (hot/spicy)

6 tbsp white wine

sea salt and freshly ground white pepper

For the mashed potatoes

4 large red potatoes

4 garlic cloves, peeled but left whole

1 bay leaf

6 tbsp extra virgin olive oil

1 tsp pimentón de la Vera picante

sea salt and freshly ground black pepper

First, you need to infuse the oil that the chicken is going to be cooked in. Heat the oil over a very gentle heat and add the garlic cloves and the bay leaf. It should take about 20 minutes to colour the garlic, very slightly. Once cooked, remove the garlic and bay leaf and set the fried garlic to one side.

Turn the heat up to high. Season the chicken, add it to the pan skin side down and fry for 10 minutes on one side – you want a nice crispy golden outside. Turn the pieces over and cook for another 5 minutes. Add the pimentón and white wine, give everything a good stir and leave to bubble gently for 5 minutes.

Meanwhile, make the mashed potatoes. Peel the potatoes and cut them into large chunks. Boil with the garlic cloves, bay leaf, 2 tablespoons of the olive oil and a pinch of salt. Once cooked, skim off the olive oil and reserve. Drain the potatoes and remove the garlic and bay leaf. Mash the potatoes with all the olive oil (both the reserved and the remaining) and the pimentón.

Spoon the mashed potatoes into the middle of a platter, place the chicken on top (skin side up) and pour over the juices. Serve with the fried garlic cloves.

DORO WAT

Ethiopia may not have a single national dish, but doro wat could stake a claim as much as any. This is a beautifully spiced stew that owes much to the spices being added in distinct layers, where flavours are reinforced in different forms and come together so well. While the passion berries are delightfully present, they by no means dominate the warm, earthy, sweet heat of the berbere spice blend or the other spices.

Serves 4

50g (2oz) niter kibbeh (page 68)

1 red onion, thinly sliced

3 garlic cloves, finely chopped

1 tbsp berbere (page 59)

½ tsp ground green cardamom seeds

1 tsp dried basil

½ tsp crushed passion berries

chilli powder, to taste (optional)

8 chicken drumsticks (or use 4 thighs)

200g (7oz) chopped canned tomatoes

1 tbsp tomato purée (paste)

200ml (7fl oz) water

4 eggs, hard-boiled and peeled

sea salt

Fry the onion in the niter kibbeh for 10–15 minutes, until the onion is soft. Add the chopped garlic, berbere, ground cardamom, dried basil, passion berries, chilli powder (if using) and chicken pieces to the fried onion and cook for 5 minutes until the chicken is beginning to cook around the edges.

Stir in the tomatoes, tomato purée and 1 teaspoon of salt and cook for 5 minutes, then add the water. Cover and cook for 45 minutes or so, until you have a thick sauce and the chicken is cooked through – add a splash of water as it cooks if it needs it. Stir in the peeled eggs and warm through for 5–10 minutes.

Serve with rice and/or flatbreads.

18ᵀᴴ-CENTURY ENGLISH CHICKEN CURRY by Annie Gray

'A receipt to curry after the Indian manner' (Martha Lloyd)

Martha Lloyd was the best friend of Jane Austen. Jane, her sister Cassandra, their mother and Martha all lived together from 1805 until Jane's death in 1817. They shared the housekeeping, and Martha kept a manuscript book of recipes, as was common at the time. It survives, and has been published in a couple of compilations. I cooked this in the kitchen at Jane Austen's House Museum in Chawton, picking it because I loved the sound of it. It's fairly typical of mid-18th-century English curry recipes, which tend to be low on spice complexity, and usually involve cooking the meat and adding spices and a thickener as for any other sauce-based dish. I like the way this one combines old world spices – turmeric and galangal – with the punch of the new world cayenne. It's a real hybrid – English tastes meet Indian culture, medieval spice meets Columbian exchange – plus the usual 18th-century tell of vast amounts of butter.

Serves 4
1 whole chicken
1 tbsp salt
225g (8oz) butter
1 onion, finely chopped
2 garlic cloves, crushed
1 orange

For the curry powder
1 tbsp galangal powder
1 tbsp ground turmeric
½ tbsp cayenne (or to taste)
3 tbsp rice flour

Joint the chicken. Put it in a pan with enough water to cover it, add the salt and bring to the boil. Simmer until almost cooked: timings depend on whether you are using joints or pieces – jointed, I give about 15 minutes for legs, 10 minutes for breast, small pieces about 5 minutes. Drain, reserving the cooking liquor.

Combine the ingredients for the curry powder in a small bowl and set aside.

Put the butter into a deep-sided pan and heat until just browning (beurre noisette). Turn down and add the onion and garlic, then stew very gently until translucent and beginning to brown: this should take 15–30 minutes, as you are essentially confiting them. Add the chicken pieces and the curry powder and stir to coat. Turn up the heat a little to brown everything off.

Add about half of the cooking liquor and bring to a very low simmer. Cook until you get a very thick sauce and the rice flour is all cooked out – about 10 minutes. Just as you serve, squeeze in the juice of half the orange. The remaining half can be sliced into neat semicircles and used as a garnish for a Regency flourish.

The sauce usually separates fairly fast and looks like one of those curries I used to eat as a student. I quite like this, and I revel in its buttery gorgeousness, but it isn't to everyone's taste. If you want to stop it separating, chuck in a couple of tablespoons of cold water (cream would probably work too) at the end and stir like crazy.

Serve with rice on the side. In the 18th century it would have been one among many dishes served simultaneously, and I usually serve with pickled vegetables, plus something green. It's useful to serve bread as well, to soak up the sauce.

CHILINDRÓN STEW

First catch your wild boar. Or find an excellent butcher. This is one of those comforting, sustaining stews that remains bright in flavour, despite the cooking time. If you can source Ñora chillies – a red, round, very mild variety, that's usually sun-dried, sometimes smoked and particularly suited to Spanish recipes – you could use them here in place of half of the sweet paprika. I like this with rice, crushed potatoes or excellent bread, and squeaky dark brassicas.

Serves 4–6

2 large red (bell) peppers

3 tbsp olive oil

800g (1lb 12oz) diced wild boar, or pork or beef

2 onions, thinly sliced

6 garlic cloves, thinly sliced

1½ tbsp sweet paprika

1 tsp hot paprika, or more or less to taste

½ tsp ground cumin

200ml (7fl oz) red wine

2 tomatoes, roughly chopped

2 tsp chopped rosemary or thyme leaves

2 bay leaves

sea salt and freshly ground black pepper

3 tbsp chopped parsley, to finish

Preheat the oven to 200°C/400°F/gas mark 6.

Roast the peppers whole for 15–20 minutes. Add to a bowl, cover and leave for a few minutes until the skins slip off easily. Peel, deseed and cut them into strips.

In a large heavy-based pan, heat the olive oil over a moderate heat, and seal the meat until coloured, in batches if needed, seasoning with a little salt and pepper. Use a slotted spoon to remove the meat, setting it aside on a plate. Leave the oil in the pan.

Add the onions to the pan and cook for 10–15 minutes until soft and lightly golden. Add the garlic, paprika, chilli (if using, see intro) and cumin and cook for a few minutes, stirring a few times.

Add half the red pepper strips along with the meat, the remaining ingredients and enough water to just cover. Bring to the boil and season to taste. Cover and place in the oven. After 15 minutes, lower the temperature to 140°C/280°F/gas mark 1 and cook for 2–3 hours until completely tender.

Allow to rest for 5 minutes, then check and adjust the seasoning if needed. Serve topped with the parsley and remaining red pepper strips.

BALUCHI-STYLE CHICKEN SAJJI by Sumayya Usmani

Use of spices in Pakistan has evolved over the years because of a confluence of cooking techniques from all of the Indian sub-continent. Migration, invasion (Arabs, Mongols), borders (Afghanistan, Iran, India, China, Central Asia), and ethnicity (there are at least ten in Pakistan) have moulded Pakistani cuisine – though a young country, our cuisine has been in the making for centuries. From royal Mughal kitchens to local regional food and a cross-cultural migration of Muslims during partition in 1947 – all this added different flavour and cooking techniques to make up what modern Pakistani cuisine is today.

This recipe (and the kunna gosht on page 196) highlights the diverse way spices are used in Pakistani cuisine and how the art of layering flavour is key to our cooking. In my family, we always cook with the idea that spices must sing on your palate first, not chilli. My cooking is rooted in flavour creation, where you extract the hidden magic of spices through different techniques, time and patience. Chilli is a back note in my cooking, and it never takes away from the main flavour of spice. To me, that's the best way to honour spices.

Sajji is the native dish of the province of Baluchistan in the west of the country – here, food is simple and cooking techniques rather rustic. Dishes usually feature spit-roasted meat or poultry, and sajji is traditionally a large leg of lamb, stuffed with pulao rice and slow-cooked over coals. The chicken version is also popular, and all over Pakistan large open-air ovens cook chickens to be topped with spicy sajji masala. My contemporary take on this dish can be an alternative to a traditional Sunday roast.

Serves 4

1.5kg (3lb 5oz) whole chicken, with skin
½ tsp salt
½ tsp freshly ground black pepper
4 garlic cloves, crushed
2 tbsp vegetable oil
2 tbsp sajji masala (page 70)
juice of 1 lemon

Rub the whole chicken with the salt, pepper and crushed garlic. Heat the oil in a large pan (big enough to hold the chicken) over a medium heat, add the chicken and seal until it is lightly browned all over. Turn the heat off and allow the chicken to cool.

Preheat the oven to 190°C/375°F/gas mark 5. Put the chicken into a roasting tray and loosely cover with foil. Roast in the oven, basting occasionally with the oil, until it is cooked through, the top is golden, and the juices run clear when the thickest part of the meat is pierced with a skewer.

Allow the chicken to rest for 5 minutes then cut it into quarters. Sprinkle the sajji masala and lemon juice over the chicken and serve with rice or naan.

JUNIPER-BRINED ROAST CHICKEN

Submerging a chicken or turkey in brine might seem like a palaver but the little effort gives such great results. First up, the texture and succulence of the meat is improved: the brine partially moves into the flesh, loosening the proteins and relaxing the meat and – as the meat tightens less as it cooks – it stays succulent. Secondly, spicing the brine gets flavour right into the heart of the bird. Here, juniper, pepper and coriander flavour the brine and thence the bird in perfect harmony, with the final sprinkling of coriander seeds bringing brighter zing to the skin.

Serves 4

For the brine

400ml (14fl oz) boiling water

40g (1½oz) coarse sea salt

2 tsp juniper berries, crushed

10 black peppercorns

2 bay leaves

4 garlic cloves, peeled but left whole

1 tbsp coriander seeds

2 strips of pared lemon zest

For the chicken

1 x 1.6kg (3lb 8oz) free-range chicken

50g (2oz) soft unsalted butter (or use 3 tbsp olive oil)

1 strip of pared lemon zest

2 garlic cloves (skin on)

1 bay leaf

water or apple juice

sea salt and freshly ground black pepper

1 tbsp coriander seeds, toasted and slightly crushed, to serve (optional)

To make the brine put all the ingredients into a large pan and simmer for 5 minutes until the salt is dissolved, then add 400ml (14fl oz) cold water and allow to cool completely.

Submerge the chicken in the brine in the pan and allow to brine for 4–8 hours.

Drain and rinse the chicken and pat the meat dry with a clean tea towel.

Preheat the oven to 220°C/425°F/gas mark 7. Rub the chicken with the butter or oil, pushing some of the butter between the flesh and skin (taking care not to tear the skin). Season generously, both inside and out, before placing in a roasting tray and adding the lemon zest, garlic and bay leaf to the cavity.

Add 1cm (½in) of water or apple juice to the bottom of the tin and put into the oven. After 15 minutes, turn the heat down to 185°C/350°F/gas mark 4 and roast for 60–70 minutes until the juices run clear when you push a skewer into a juicy part of the leg.

Allow the chicken to rest for 15 minutes before carving, straining any cooking juices to serve with the carved chicken or to make gravy. Serve sprinkled with the coriander seeds (if using) to taste.

JANSSON'S TEMPTATION

You could give me this wonderful Swedish potato dish every day for a week and I'd not complain. Variations are many – I often make this with celeriac, or all dairy rather than part stock, or leave out the breadcrumbs if I can't be arsed – and this is my current favourite way. The spices are all widely used in Scandinavia and come together beautifully. It isn't critical that the pepper is white, but I like it that way. This makes as good a main with dark, irony brassicas or sprouting broccoli as it does a side to roast lamb.

Serves 4

½ tsp caraway seeds
½ tsp dill seeds
½ tsp anise seed
½ tsp celery seeds
½ tsp white peppercorns
1 tbsp olive oil
8 anchovy fillets, plus a little of their oil
3 medium onions, very thinly sliced
800g (1lb 12oz) potatoes, peeled and thinly sliced
200ml (7fl oz) chicken or vegetable stock
pinch of ground white pepper
150ml (5fl oz) double (heavy) cream
60g (2¼oz) breadcrumbs

Preheat the oven to 200°C/400°F/gas mark 6.

Toast the spices in a dry pan until fragrant, shaking the pan to prevent burning. Reduce to a powder in a spice grinder or with a pestle and mortar.

Heat the oil in a large, ovenproof frying pan over a low–medium heat. Add a tablespoon of the anchovy oil and then the onions and cook over a low heat, stirring occasionally, until they are very soft. Remove the onions from the pan.

Add layers of potato to the pan up to halfway. Carefully pour in the stock. Spread the onions evenly on top and dot with the anchovies. Season with a pinch of white pepper, then add the remaining potato in layers, followed by the cream. Press the potatoes into the creamy stock.

Place in the oven and cook for 20 minutes, pressing the potatoes into the liquid a couple of times. Remove from the oven. Scatter with the spice mix, then the breadcrumbs. Add a little milk to top up if needed. Reduce the oven temperature to 180°C/350°F/gas mark 4 and bake for another 30–40 minutes until the top is golden and the potatoes cooked.

DUCK, PORK AND BUTTER BEAN PAELLA

What most of us see as a Spanish classic is more accurately of Valencia, a region occupying the middle of Spain's eastern coast. I love paella's many incarnations, including this special version without the familiar seafood. Behold the power of a tweak of paprika and a pinch of saffron. If you aren't confident with a chopper, ask your butcher to prepare the ribs and duck for you. And yes, by all means use chicken instead of the duck.

Serves 4–6

3 tbsp olive oil

2 duck legs, each chopped into 4 pieces through the bone

500g (1lb 2oz) pork ribs, chopped into small pieces across the bone

1 onion, finely diced

1 red (bell) pepper, finely chopped

3 garlic cloves, thinly sliced

generous pinch of sweet paprika

200g (7oz) canned chopped tomatoes

good pinch of saffron, soaked in a little warm water for about 10 minutes

800ml (1¾ pints) hot chicken stock or water

400g (14oz) paella rice

150g (5oz) green beans, trimmed

100g (3½oz) jarred roasted red peppers, drained (piquillo peppers are nice if you can find them)

400g (14oz) can butter beans, drained and rinsed

sea salt

lemon wedges, to serve (or use sour orange)

Place a paella pan over a medium heat. Add the oil, then add the meat and cook for about 10 minutes, turning frequently, until nicely brown all over. Push the meat to the edges of the pan and add the onion, pepper and garlic to the pan and cook to soften for 5–10 minutes. Stir in the paprika, chopped tomatoes and the saffron with its soaking water. Cook for about 5 minutes, then stir the fried meat into the vegetables, mixing well. Add the stock and bring to a simmer, adding salt to taste.

Evenly sprinkle the rice into the stock, then increase the heat to high and let the paella cook for about 10 minutes. Scatter the green beans, peppers and butter beans over the surface of the paella, reduce the heat and cook for 10–15 minutes more, without stirring, or until the rice is just cooked and the liquid has been fully absorbed.

Remove from the heat and rest for at least 5 minutes. Serve straight from the pan, scraping up the bottom bits, with some lemon or sour orange wedges.

BABI GULING

Now that I no longer keep pigs, I rarely eat pork. When I do, I like to know who has raised them and how, given how dreadfully these beautifully bright creatures are routinely kept. On the rare days I eat pork, this phenomenal Balinese dish is so often what I go for.

While this recipe is loyal to the spirit and flavour of a classic babi guling, it differs in a few material ways. First up, babi guling translates as 'turning pig', reflecting it traditionally being cooked on a spit over an open fire. Secondly, I have adapted the dish from the traditional suckling pig to use the belly from a pig that has lived a happy, long life, freely expressing its pigginess in its many characteristic ways. Lastly, the skin is traditionally rubbed with ground turmeric, which gives a wonderful golden crackling; I confess to preferring it with just salt. By all means bring any or all of those rules back.

Serves 4

1.2kg (2lb 9oz) pork belly joint with skin on

1 batch of bumbu paste (page 61)

3 tbsp sunflower or coconut oil

250ml (9fl oz) boiling water

200ml (7fl oz) coconut milk

200ml (7fl oz) chicken stock or water

sea salt and freshly ground black pepper

Preheat the oven to 180°C/350°F/gas mark 4.

Pat the pork dry with a clean tea towel, then slash five or six cuts, 1cm (½in) deep, into the flesh side with a sharp knife.

Mix half the bumbu with 1 tablespoon of oil and rub into the flesh side of the pork. Roll the belly up into a Swiss roll and secure tightly using three or four loops of butcher's string. Rub ½ teaspoon of salt into the skin.

Place the pork on a rack set over a roasting tray with the boiling water in. Roast for 1 hour 15 minutes until you can insert a skewer into the middle of the pork and no pink juices run out.

Increase the heat to 240°C/460°F/gas mark 9 and roast for a further 15–30 minutes until the skin is golden and crackled all over. Remove from the oven and allow it to rest for about 25 minutes in a warm place.

While the pork is resting, fry the remaining bumbu paste in 2 tablespoons oil for 5 minutes or so until it starts to stick and brown a little. Stir in the coconut milk and stock and simmer for 10 minutes until thickened slightly.

Remove the crackling from the pork and break it into pieces. Slice the pork and serve with the crackling, the sauce, and a little of the roasting liquid spooned over. Enjoy with a small bowl of sambal (page 88) and rice.

KUNNA GOSHT by Sumayya Usmani

Kunna gosht is a dish that will be familiar to those who have had nihari – it's very similar, but there's a subtle variation in spice. Hailing from the Punjabi town of Chinot in the eastern part of Pakistan (known for its beautiful hand-carved rosewood furniture), this rich and extravagant Punjabi wedding dish is made of slow-cooked lamb or mutton shanks and garam masala. It's eaten topped with ginger, coriander leaves and more spice, and served with hot naans.

Serves 10–12

4 tbsp vegetable oil

2 tbsp ghee

1 large onion, thinly sliced

2.5cm (1in) fresh ginger, peeled and finely grated

½ tbsp crushed garlic

2kg (4lb 8oz) leg of lamb (or 2 large shanks) chopped into 5–6 pieces with marrow exposed, or 3 large lamb shanks, each cut into 2, marrow exposed

1 tsp red chilli powder

2 tsp salt, or to taste

1 batch of garam masala (page 64)

1½ tbsp Kashmiri chilli powder

1 litre (2 pints) water

2 tbsp plain (all-purpose) flour, mixed with a little water to form a paste

To garnish

large handful of coriander (cilantro), roughly chopped

5cm (2in) fresh ginger, peeled and cut into julienne

4 thin green chillies, finely chopped

4 large lemons, cut into wedges

10 medium onions, deep-fried until medium brown

Heat the oil and ghee together in a large heavy-based pan over a medium heat. When hot, add the onion, ginger and garlic and cook for a few minutes, stirring until the raw smell disappears. Add the lamb and fry until the meat is sealed. Add the red chilli powder, salt and about 3–4 tablespoons of the garam masala, reserving 2–3 tablespoons for the end. Fry until the masala is fragrant; if it is sticking to the pan add a splash of water as you go.

Add the Kashmiri chilli powder and stir until the meat is evenly coated in all the masalas. Pour in the measured water to cover the meat – you may need to add more water to ensure the meat is completely covered. Reduce the heat slightly to medium–low, then cover and cook for about 45 minutes–1 hour. Keep checking to make sure that the meat is not boiling hard.

After about an hour, remove 250ml (9fl oz) of the liquid from the pan and beat in the flour paste, before returning it back to the pan. Stir in evenly, then cover the pan with the lid, reduce the heat to very low and cook gently for a further 2 hours, or until the meat falls off the bone.

Serve topped with coriander, the remaining garam masala and finely julienned ginger, chopped green chillies, lemon wedges and deep-fried onions in small bowls on the side. Enjoy with naan, crusty bread or rice.

BARBECUE RIBS

The barbecue sauce on page 96 is a beautifully spiced, hot, sweet, sour delight that works as well when in cooked recipes like this as added to burgers; that said, cooking changes the emphasis of the flavours just a little, so by all means serve with a little more sauce if you fancy. I always mean to serve this with something virtuous and green but it's always a match and a beer.

Serves 2–3, or just me if I can get away with it

1kg (2lb 4oz) pork ribs

⅓ batch of barbecue sauce (page 96)

sea salt and freshly ground black pepper

Preheat the oven to 150°C/300°F/gas mark 2.

Place the ribs into a roasting tray large enough to accommodate them in a single layer, close-ish but not jammed in. Season well with salt and pepper. Spoon the spicy sauce over the ribs. Cover the tin in foil and cook for 2 hours.

Turn the heat up to 180°C/350°F/gas mark 4. Take the dish out and spoon on some of the sauce from the base over the ribs. Cook for 15–20 minutes more without the foil: keep an eye on it to avoid burning.

BIGOS by Zuza Zak

Bigos is the quintessential Polish winter stew. A traditional bigos is a hunter's stew with plenty of meat, sauerkraut, wild mushrooms and prunes, cooked over three days (and reheated for days to come too). This is not a subtle dish: bigos is strong and bold. The predominant flavouring is allspice, which manages to cut through all the other strong flavours in the dish. Ironically, allspice is called 'ziele angielskie' in Polish, which literally translates as the 'English herb'. It's funny, because this spice is used far more in Polish cooking; almost every Polish soup requires a few allspice berries. This is a simplified version of bigos, for a more traditional one see my cookbook Polska: New Polish Cooking.

Makes about 15 servings

100g (3½oz) dried wild mushrooms

5 tbsp rapeseed oil

400g (14oz) pork belly, cubed

1 onion, finely chopped

400g (14oz) stewing beef, cubed

10 allspice berries

2 bay leaves

1.5kg (3lb 5oz) sauerkraut, drained

300ml (10fl oz) red wine

500ml (1 pint) beef stock

100g (3½oz) closed-cup mushrooms, chopped

150g (5oz) Polish sausage, cubed

150g (5oz) prunes, pitted

1 tbsp soy sauce

salt and freshly ground white and black pepper

Wash the dried mushrooms under running water, then place in a bowl and cover with boiling water. After 2 minutes, drain and wash again under running water. Return to the bowl, pour boiling water over them again and allow to stand for 30 minutes.

Meanwhile, in a very large pan, heat 2 tablespoons of the rapeseed oil over a high heat and fry the pork belly for about 5 minutes, browning evenly. Turn the heat down to low, add the onion and the beef and fry for another couple of minutes. Add the allspice berries, bay leaves and sauerkraut and pour over 100ml (3½fl oz) of the wine. Season with white and black pepper, then bring to the boil and allow to simmer gently for a couple of minutes.

Add the stock. Cut the now-rehydrated wild mushrooms into slivers and add them to the pan along with the liquid, but keeping back the sediment in the bottom of the bowl. Cook for 2 hours over a low heat, stirring regularly and adding a splash of water if it ever looks dry. Allow the bigos to cool and keep in the fridge or a cool place overnight.

The next day, pour over the rest of the wine and bring the bigos to a simmer once again.

Start frying the mushrooms and Polish sausage in batches. Add each batch to the pan as they turn brown. Finally, add the prunes and cook altogether for further 2 hours. Keep checking on the bigos and if it ever begins to look dry, add a splash of water. It should always be moist.

Add the soy sauce, taste and season with salt and both the peppers to taste at the end. Serve with rye bread or dill potatoes.

PASTILLA

This North African pie is commonly made with meat or fish, but the spicing works beautifully with squash too. Butternut is great here, but if you can get either Crown Prince or uchiki kuri, you'll be glad you did. The traditional warqa pastry is delightfully substituted here for the similar and widely available filo. While ras el hanout may drive the flavour, the key ingredients of this recipe are equal amounts of confidence and care: take your time with the pastry but don't be tentative.

This is as good cold for lunch the next day as it is warm, 20 minutes out of the oven.

Serves 4–6

800g (1lb 12oz) butternut squash, peeled, deseeded and cut into 2–3cm (1in) chunks

1 tbsp olive oil

2 onions, finely chopped

80g (3oz) melted butter

3 garlic cloves, finely chopped

1 tbsp tomato purée (paste)

2 tsp ras al hanout (page 69)

150ml (5fl oz) vegetable stock or water

75g (2½oz) chopped almonds or pistachios

75g (2½oz) dried dates, apricots or raisins, roughly chopped

3 eggs, beaten

small bunch of coriander (cilantro), finely chopped

5 large sheets of filo pastry

1 tbsp icing (confectioners') sugar

½ tsp ground cinnamon

sea salt and freshly ground black pepper

harissa (page 66), to serve (optional)

Preheat the oven to 180°C/350°F/gas mark 4. Grease a springform tin, about 22cm (9in) in diameter, with a little butter.

Toss the squash in the olive oil and roast on a tray for about 20 minutes or so until tender.

Meanwhile, in a large pan over a low heat, cook the onions in 1 tablespoon of the melted butter for 15 minutes until soft. Add the garlic, tomato purée and the ras el hanout and cook for a minute more. Add the roasted squash to the pan, along with the stock or water. Season, bring to the boil, and simmer for about 5 minutes. Stir in the nuts and dried fruit, then add the eggs and gently cook until it resembles loose scrambled eggs. Add the coriander, season with salt and pepper to taste and put to one side.

Take a sheet of filo pastry and brush it with melted butter. Drape it over the greased tin, gently pushing into the corners. Repeat with another sheet of filo, this time placing it at a right angle to the first. Repeat with the next two sheets of filo to form a large pastry case with no tears.

Spoon the mixture into a round heap in the centre of the pastry, ease it towards the edge, then take the corners of the pastry and wrap it over the filling to encase it, pressing a little to persuade it into a slightly domed cake shape. Lay the final filo sheet on top, scrunch it to fit, brush with butter and tuck under any corners.

Bake in the oven for about 30 minutes until the pastry is a crisp and golden brown. Remove from the oven and allow to cool a little before dusting with the icing sugar and the cinnamon.

Serve with harissa on the side, if you like.

SWEET THINGS

APPLE, QUINCE AND STAR ANISE TARTE TATIN

Having found my tarte often stuck, I've developed a few rules from which
I never waver: the pan must be non-stick (mostly, I use a Netherton Prospector
pan or a shallow Le Creuset); I don't let much time pass between hob and oven;
and I turn the tarte out before it cools too much. I have to tell you, I'm happy
with bought puff pastry. I almost always make this with only star anise as it
complements rather than sings over the top of the quince; if you are making
this with just apples, allow me to steer you towards cinnamon berries, verbena
berries and Ethiopian passion berries – or a combination of – as well as the
more familiar flavours of cinnamon or cardamom.

Serves 4–6

150g (5oz) caster (superfine)
sugar

2 whole star anise, ground

80g (3oz) salted butter

4 apples, peeled, cored and
quartered

2 quince, peeled, cored and
quartered

250g (9oz) all-butter puff
pastry

Preheat the oven to 160°C/320°F/gas mark 3.

Put a 20cm (8in) shallow, non-stick, ovenproof pan on the hob over a medium
heat, and add the sugar, star anise and 60g (2¼oz) of the butter to it, stirring
to blend thoroughly as they melt. Up the heat a little, stir occasionally, and
allow the buttery sugar to turn to a brown caramel.

Warm the remaining butter in a separate pan over a low heat.

Arrange the apple and quince pieces around the edge of the pan of caramel,
then in an inner circle. Cook for a couple of minutes, then brush with the
melted butter. Remove from the heat.

Cut a circle from the pastry that is 2cm (¾in) or so larger than the pan's
diameter. Place it on top of the fruit and tuck in the edges down the inside of
the pan. Use a sharp knife cut a couple of little slits in the top to allow steam
to escape.

Place in the oven and cook for 25–30 minutes: the pastry should be golden and
crisp. Allow to cool for 5 minutes, before placing a plate over the pan, and
(using oven gloves) inverting the whole in one swift movement. Carefully
remove the pan. Use a spoon to move any stubborn bits of fruit or caramel
from the pan to the tarte. Serve with sour cream or yoghurt.

CARDAMOM POACHED PEARS

This is more of a template than a recipe; the pears might be nectarines or quince, the wine substituted for cider, the cardamom for star anise, and the bay for lemon verbena. You get the picture. It's a great way with fruit and a reviver of even the most reluctant underripe fruit. It's also at the heart of an exceptional trifle (page 234).

Serves 4–6

1 bottle of dry white wine

250g (9oz) sugar

12 small pears

12 cardamom pods, seeds only

1 bay leaf, cracked

Add the wine and sugar to a pan and bring slowly to a simmer, stirring to dissolve the sugar.

While it warms up, peel the pears.

When the wine reaches a simmer, use a spoon to lower the pears in, adding the cardamom seeds and bay leaf. Lower to a whisper of a simmer, and allow to gently tickle away until the pears take the point of a sharp knife: this might be 10 minutes or 20 depending on the ripeness of the fruit.

Serve the pears warm with a little of the sweet liquor and ice cream: the bastani (page 227) is very good with it.

RICE PUDDING WITH SWEET DUKKAH

As a kid, I would occasionally find myself daydreaming about tinned rice pudding. There were apricot and apple versions that I loved as much as the original. If there was a tin to be retrieved from the spidery dark larder, I'd sit on the front step on a sunny day, spoon dipping into the can of cold ambrosia, trying not to cut my finger on the upturned lid, and be as happy as when Kenny scored the goal that won the European Cup. I still love tinned rice pudding, but this is quite the upgrade.

I make this to enjoy hot straight from the oven, and as much for little me to enjoy the leftovers cold the next day. Sweet garam masala is a great alternative to the dukkah, as is a pairing of ground green cardamom and mace. I've also made this with barista oat milk, which gives a nice maltiness.

Serves 4–6

1 bay leaf

2 strips of pared orange zest

650ml (1½ pints) whole milk

120g (4oz) arborio rice, rinsed

40g (1½oz) caster (superfine) sugar

10g (¼oz) demerara sugar

1 batch of sweet dukkah (page 63)

Place the bay leaf and orange zest in a medium pan with the milk and bring to a simmer. Add the rice, stir and bring back up to the boil briefly, and then down to a gentle simmer. Cook, stirring often. It should take 25–35 minutes for the rice to cook.

Remove the bay leaf and orange zest, stir in the sugar, and add a touch more milk if needed.

Turn the grill (broiler) to high. Pour the creamy rice into an ovenproof dish, sprinkle with the demerara and flash under the grill until a just-browning skin forms. Sprinkle with as much or little sweet dukkah as takes your fancy.

SWEET GARAM MASALA ROAST FIGS

For a few short weeks as summer and autumn hold hands, cardboard trays of figs appear in the shops and markets where I live: this makes me very happy. Occasionally I make a tart with them; once in a while they find a home in an ice cream or trifle, but most often I make this: the work of minutes delivering such pleasure. It's also an excuse to enjoy the quiet pleasure of a knife slicing through a succulent fig; like writing on a banana skin with a biro.

Serves 4–6

12 figs, halved top to bottom

2 tbsp runny honey

2–3 tbsp sweet garam masala (page 64)

Preheat the oven to 160°C/320°F/gas mark 3.

Place the fig halves cut side up on a tray. Drizzle with honey and sprinkle with the garam masala. Place in the oven and cook for 30 minutes or so until soft and giving: check after 25 minutes as the timing depends on the size and succulence of the figs. Serve with yoghurt, labneh or sweet long pepper cream (page 226).

Pictured opposite.

GARAM MASALA PLUMS

I've never been one for the grand plan or 'what do you want to be doing in five years': I'm ever more convinced that happy accident drives most things, and is largely what separates the lucky from those floating on a raft in treacherous seas. Here's a micro example: when testing whether plums might take to the sweet garam masala figs treatment (above) I accidentally used the wrong garam masala – so I straightened it out with a little sugar and cinnamon and my god the black cardamom and other earthinesses in the savoury garam masala work so well here. As simple as it is delicious.

Serves 4–6

1kg (2lb 4oz) plums, halved and stoned

2 tbsp savoury garam masala (page 64)

1 tbsp caster (superfine) sugar

1 tbsp ground cinnamon

Preheat the oven to 160°C/320°F/gas mark 3.

Place the plum halves cut side up on a tray. Sprinkle with the garam masala, sugar and cinnamon. Place in the oven and cook for 30 minutes or so until soft and giving.

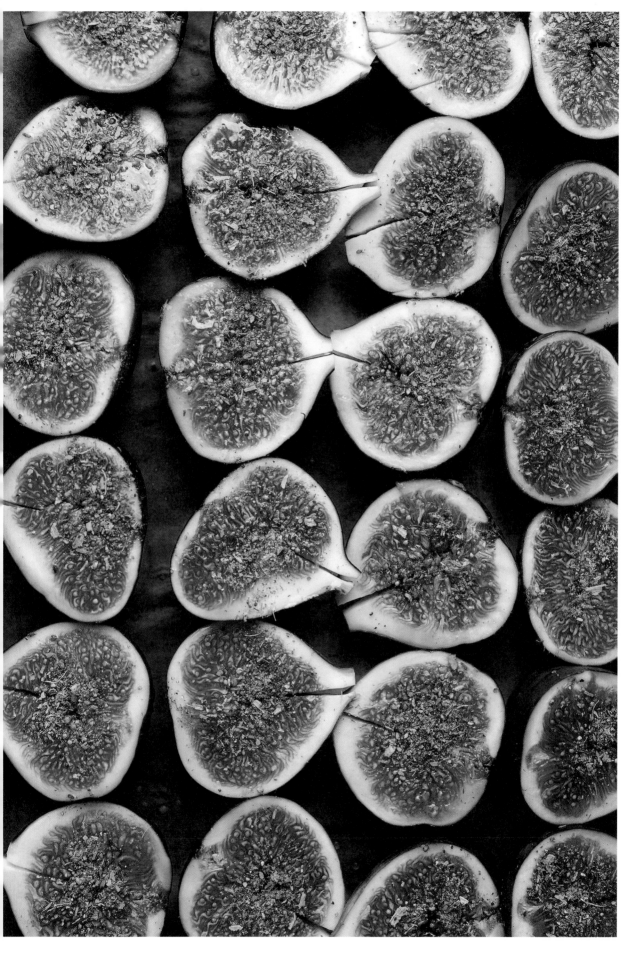

BLUEBERRY AND CORIANDER CLAFOUTIS

This may sound like a peculiar combination, but blueberries and coriander share a flavour compound, and the coriander just sparks the blueberries' intensity perfectly. There are three critical things to clafoutis: a light touch when whisking the batter, a blisteringly hot oven and don't grind the coriander too fine – it's best as chewy intense nuggets. This is also excellent cold for breakfast.

Serves 6

70g (2½oz) plain (all-purpose) flour, plus a little extra for dusting

½ tsp salt

330ml (11fl oz) whole milk

2 tsp vanilla extract

2 eggs

40g (1½oz) caster (superfine) sugar

200g (7oz) blueberries

2 tsp coriander seeds, coarsely ground

15g (½oz) unsalted butter, chilled and cut into small pieces, plus a little extra for greasing

1 tbsp icing (confectioners') sugar, for dusting

1 tsp cocoa powder, for dusting (optional)

Preheat the oven to 220°C/430°F/gas mark 7. Butter a gratin or baking dish (about 28 x 20cm/11 x 8in) and dust it lightly with flour.

Sift the flour and salt into a bowl and whisk in half the milk and vanilla until smooth. Add the eggs one at a time, whisking briefly after each addition. Whisk in the sugar and remaining milk.

Scatter the blueberries into the dish, add half of the coriander, pour over the batter and dot with the butter. Place the dish on a baking sheet and bake until puffed up and golden, about 25 minutes. Remove from the oven, leave to cool slightly and dust with icing sugar, the remaining coriander and the cocoa (if using) just before serving.

A RUSSIAN GOGOL-MOGOL WITH RYE AND CORIANDER by Alissa Timoshkina

This recipe is inspired by my childhood favourite food – a whipped egg yolk with sugar that I would eat with a slice of Russian rye bread, and that my granny (bless her) would whip by hand to the most perfect creamy fluffy texture.

Serves 4

3 egg yolks

1 whole egg

4 tsp caster (superfine) sugar

1 tsp coriander seeds

4 slices of sweet rye bread (Russian or Lithuanian rye or pumpernickel)

30g (1oz) unsalted butter

2 tbsp fragrant runny honey

¼ tsp grated nutmeg, plus extra to serve

½ tsp ground cinnamon

1 tsp vanilla extract

zest and juice of ½ orange

Put the yolks and the egg into a bowl with the sugar and whisk using an electric whisk at high speed for 8–10 minutes until soft peaks form.

In the meantime, place a frying pan over a medium heat and toast the coriander seeds for a few minutes until they brown and release their aroma. Set aside to cool a little then give them a good bash around in a pestle and mortar. The spice will double in volume, now yielding approximately 2 teaspoons.

Cut the crusts off the bread (reserve them to make some croutons) and roughly rip the bread into bite-sized chunks.

Melt the butter in the same pan, then fry the bread with the honey, half the toasted coriander, the nutmeg and the cinnamon for about 2 minutes until all the butter is absorbed. Finally add the vanilla extract, half the orange zest and all the juice. Taste and adjust the spices or honey to your taste.

To serve, place a spoonful of the custard in four small glasses, and layer alternately with the fragrant sticky bread mix. Sprinkle with coriander seed, the remaining orange zest and a generous scratch of nutmeg.

LEBKUCHEN

There are many things I would do for the offer of a well-timed biscuit. Festive as they are, lebkuchen are never not welcome out of season. There is – thank heavens – a fine tradition of spiced biscuits round the world, including biscochitos of New Mexico, Germany's lebkuchen and Finland's spiced gingerbread, which share a common thread of celebration; I salute them all, and encourage you to go forth in greedy inquisitiveness.

For the gluten intolerant, or if you fancy, the plain flour can be substituted with oat flour and/or ground almonds. Some lebkuchen have dried peel in; I'm not interested. They can be iced; I can't be arsed.

Makes about 30

150g (5oz) honey

60g (2¼oz) unsalted butter, softened

450g (1lb) plain (all-purpose) flour (see intro), plus extra for dusting

2 tbsp lebkuchengewürz (page 67)

3 good pinches of salt

½ tsp baking powder

½ tsp bicarbonate of soda (baking soda)

170g (6oz) soft dark brown sugar

finely grated zest of 1 lemon

2 large eggs, briefly whisked

Pour the honey and butter into a small pan and warm over a low heat, stirring to combine.

Put all the remaining ingredients except the eggs in a bowl and stir in the honey butter. Slowly add the eggs while stirring: a tacky dough should come together. Cover the bowl with a damp cloth and rest in the fridge for 1 hour.

Preheat the oven to 180°C/350°F/gas mark 4 and line 2 or 3 baking sheets with baking parchment.

Lightly flour the work surface and roll the dough out to around 7–8mm (¼–½in) thick. Use a cookie cutter to make biscuits of whatever shape you favour. Place on the baking sheets and bake in the centre of the oven for about 12 minutes until very slightly risen; catch them before they darken too much. Cool on a wire rack.

They will store for 4–5 days in an airtight container.

WATTLESEED SHORTBREAD

This is my default shortbread recipe – it's shorter than my old man's patience – and while the dough may pretend it doesn't want to come together, have faith. It is promiscuously adaptable to other spices, but wattleseed just might take the biscuit. Its chocolate-hazelnut-coffee flavour is so very good here, especially if you have it with a coffee.

Makes 12–16

200g (7oz) unsalted butter

100g (3½oz) caster (superfine) sugar, plus extra for sprinkling

300g (10oz) plain (all-purpose) flour

pinch of salt

3 tsp wattleseed

Preheat the oven to 160°C/320°F/gas mark 3.

Cream the butter with the sugar. Sift in the flour, salt and wattleseed and combine until it comes together. Roll out on a lightly floured surface to around 5–7mm (¼in) thick and use a small cookie cutter to create circles of shortbread.

Place the shortbread circles on a baking sheet and bake until just thinking about turning lightly brown – about 15–20 minutes. Sprinkle with a little more sugar and allow to cool for 10 minutes before transferring to a wire rack, where they will firm up as they cool.

BUÑUELOS WITH PILONCILLO SYRUP by Nicola Miller

Brought to the Americas by Spanish colonizers in the 16th century, anise has become one of the flavours I associate most with Mexico. Used to flavour pan de muertos, mole poblano, teas made to soothe babies with colic (not dissimilar in flavour to the fennel granules I used to give my children) and biscocho, I think of it as the clarinet of the spice world. Its liquorice notes are bright, confident and throaty as they wind their way through this recipe for little fried dough fritters drenched in heavy, aromatic syrup. The syrup is made with piloncillo – an unrefined cane sugar, rich and dark, and usually sold as a solid cone or a 'little loaf' – the juice and zest from orange and lime, anise seed and cinnamon. These are bold flavours.

Typically eaten over Christmas and the New Year in Mexico, buñuelos are something I eat year-round here in the UK. There are a lot of variations (in southern Mexico, they resemble little doughnuts), but in the north where I once lived, they are flattened into little discs of dough before being fried and drenched in a piloncillo syrup. We'd buy them from street vendors, but many Mexicans fry them at home. You'll need to be ready to eat buñuelos as they emerge from the pan; puffy and red-hot is when they are at their best. When Jona Lewie said he was always in the kitchen at parties, it was probably because his host was frying buñuelos. They draw people in.

Makes 10–12

300g (10oz) plain (all-purpose) flour, plus extra for dusting

1 tbsp golden caster (superfine) sugar

½ tsp table salt

1 tsp baking powder

1 large egg

1 tsp vanilla extract

15g (½oz) unsalted butter or lard, melted

about 100–125ml (3½–4fl oz) warm water

800ml (1¾ pints) vegetable oil, for frying

granulated sugar, for dusting

To make the buñuelos, place the flour, sugar, salt and baking powder in a large bowl, stir together then make a well in the centre. Break the egg into a small bowl and beat until frothy, then add the vanilla extract and melted butter (or lard) to it. Pour the wet ingredients into the dry and rub the mixture together with your fingers until the dough resembles a mass of rough breadcrumbs.

Now start to add the warm water, a little at a time, until you have a smooth, pale, slightly tacky dough. You may not need the whole quantity of water, so go carefully. Flour your surface and turn the dough out on to it. Lightly knead the dough for 5 minutes, then wrap it in clingfilm (plastic wrap) and place in the fridge to rest for half an hour.

While the dough is resting, make your syrup. Place the orange juice, piloncillo sugar, cinnamon stick and anise seed in a heavy-based pan and cook over a medium–high heat for a few minutes until the piloncillo dissolves. As the piloncillo softens, I encourage you to break it up by bashing at it with a wooden spoon. Stir frequently and never leave the pan unattended because it tends to bubble up. After 10 minutes of cooking, add the lime and orange zest, then boil for another 10 minutes, or until the syrup thinly coats a spoon. Strain and set aside while you fry the buñuelos.

Continued overleaf

For the syrup

200ml (7fl oz) fresh orange juice

300g (10oz) piloncillo sugar (panela)

½ cinnamon stick

½ tsp anise seed

1 tsp grated lime zest (save the juice)

1 tsp grated orange zest

Pour the oil into a deep, wide pan or deep-fat fryer and heat to 190°C/375°F.

While your oil is heating, remove the dough from the fridge, re-flour your surface and divide the dough into 10 equal-sized balls. Now roll each one as thinly as you can into a circle without tearing the dough. Obviously, you will need to make sure they fit your pan, so don't worry if you need to make 12 slightly smaller circles – what is important is that they are very thin.

Fry the circles one by one, monitoring the temperature of the oil to keep it constant, and flipping the fritters over when their underneath is golden brown, bubbly and crisp. Drain each one on a piece of kitchen paper and sprinkle with granulated sugar. Keep frying until they are all done.

Serve the buñuelos by breaking them into pieces and dividing their shards between plates before pouring the orange-anise syrup over the top, plus a squeeze of lime juice if you like. I like to eat them with a cup of Mexican hot chocolate for a winter breakfast, and they are really good with fried apples. You can keep buñuelos for later and warm them up in the oven, but I tend to eat them straight out of the fryer. Have everyone waiting around the table before you begin to cook them. They don't like waiting around for stragglers. You can reheat the syrup if it gets very thick when it's cold.

MINCEMEAT

As with marmalade, George Benson and cycling, mincemeat is one of those things I love very much, but want only very occasionally. I find I am insistent on the quality of these deep infrequent pleasures even more than the regular ones: I hope you'll find this an excellent upgrade on the familiar. The dried berries, the quince and the spices uplift everything, and the use of vegetarian suet and absence of butter make this perfect for those who eat a plant-based diet. If you have just made a but-there's-no-candied-peel face: trust me.

Makes about 1 litre (2 pints)

375g (13oz) raisins

180g (6oz) dried cranberries

150g (5oz) dried blueberries

6 dried apricots, chopped

2 cooking apples, peeled and grated

1 quince, grated

220g (8oz) light muscovado sugar

40g (1½oz) honey

4 tsp sweet garam masala (page 64)

1 tsp ground ginger

100g (3½oz) vegetarian suet

200ml (7fl oz) krupnik (page 252)

Place everything except the krupnik in a large pan and bring to a slow simmer. Cook, stirring often for about 20 minutes; the apples should dissolve and the entirety softly surrender into glossy relaxation.

Allow to cool for 15 minutes before stirring the krupnik through. Transfer to a sterilized jar and store somewhere cool and dark. It will keep for a long time, but you'll finish it before you ever find out.

APPLE, MINCEMEAT AND FENNEL CRUMBLE

If I am good for anything, it is for making crumble. Old pal and ex-River Cottage chef Tim Maddams introduced me to the pleasure of the olive oil crumble many years ago and I rarely deviate to other fats now. Here, fennel brightens the topping: a teaspoon or two of ground cardamom, allspice or star anise work differently well if you prefer.

I often leave the fruit layer to speak for itself, but a top coat of mincemeat, or a generous dusting of qalat daqqa, sweet garam masala, Lebkuchengewürz or five-spice can be perfect if I'm in the mood.

Serves 6–8

350g (12oz) oats
120g (4oz) sugar
100ml (3½fl oz) olive oil
3 tbsp fennel seeds
5 cooking apples
100ml (3½fl oz) water
280g (9½oz) mincemeat
(page 221)

Preheat the oven to 165°C/340°F/gas mark 3.

Whizz 250g (9oz) of the oats in a food processor until it forms a rough flour. Add the sugar, then, with the blender on low, drizzle the oil in slowly: it should come together into a fudgy delight. Stir in the rest of the oats and the fennel seeds.

Peel the apples and cut the flesh into thin pieces. Add them to a baking dish of about 23 x 18cm (9 x 7in). Slowly pour in the water: this will part-steam the apples and keep the resulting purée lush. Use a spoon to spread the mincemeat over the apples.

Top with the crumble and place in the oven. Cook for 30 minutes or so, until bubbling at the edges and the top is lightly brown. Serve with too much sour or double (heavy) cream.

QALAT DAQQA PLUM CAKE

I have no interest in Victoria sponge. As the years click by, my resolve for dense cake deepens. Here, the oats, almonds and oil bring body and nuttiness and draw the fruit and spice into the heart of the cake beautifully. This is really good with apples and quince, rhubarb, and raspberries instead of the plums, and do try sweet garam masala or ras el hanout instead of the qalat daqqa.

Serves 6–8

125ml (4fl oz) olive oil

140g (4¾oz) caster (superfine) sugar

3 eggs

190g (6½oz) oats, blitzed in a processor to a coarse powder

50g (2oz) ground almonds

1½ tsp baking powder

2 tbsp qalat daqqa (page 69)

4–5 plums, halved and stoned

sprinkle of demerara sugar (optional)

Preheat the oven to 180°C/350°F/gas mark 4 and line the base of a deep, loose-bottomed 20cm (8in) round cake tin with baking parchment.

Whisk the oil and sugar together thoroughly. Add the eggs, stirring in well.

Mix together the oat flour, ground almonds, baking powder and qalat daqqa. Stir into the batter until full incorporated, then pour into the cake tin. Lay the plums on top, cut side up, and scatter with the demerera, if using.

Bake for 50 minutes, then test with a cocktail stick or cake tester; when it comes out clean, the cake is cooked. Allow more time in 5-minute increments if required.

Allow the cake to cool a little, before running a knife around the edge of the cake and releasing it (with the base) from the tin.

Serve with whichever cream or yoghurt takes your fancy.

RAS EL HANOUT AND CHOCOLATE BANANA BREAD
by Nargisse Benkabbou

I heard about banana bread for the first time about 12 years ago when I moved to London. I have to say, I was very confused by the sound of it initially. Why would anyone want to include a ripe banana in their bread? Little did I know how much I would love it! I immediately found the particular texture of the bread and its charming aromas quite addictive. As I was falling in love with the London dining scene, I also fell in love with banana bread and more particularly, with the kind that includes a generous amount of chocolate in the batter. I ordered it countless times in coffee shops before I started experimenting with baking my own at home. A few years down the road and I had developed my own foolproof recipe, with chocolate chips and a generous amount of ras el hanout.

Serves 8

260g (9oz) plain
(all-purpose) flour

1½ tsp baking powder

½ tsp bicarbonate of soda
(baking soda)

2 tsp ras el hanout (page 69)

1 tsp salt

2 large eggs

180g (6oz) soft light brown
sugar

120g (4oz) butter, melted,
plus extra for greasing

60ml (4 tbsp) black tea

2 tsp vanilla extract

320g (11oz) ripe banana
mash (from 2–3 ripe
bananas)

140g (5oz) dark chocolate
chips

For the ras el hanout sugar

3 tbsp caster (superfine)
sugar

1 tsp ras el hanout (page 69)

Preheat the oven to 180°C/350°F/gas mark 4 and lightly butter and line a 900g (2lb) loaf tin.

In a large bowl, whisk together the flour, baking powder, bicarbonate of soda, ras el hanout and salt until combined.

In another bowl, whisk the eggs and brown sugar together until well combined. Add the melted butter, black tea and vanilla extract and whisk again, then add the mashed bananas and whisk again until combined.

Pour the dry ingredients into the wet ingredients and gently mix together using a spatula. Do not overmix the batter because this will make the bread gummy (it's totally fine if we can still see some flecks of flour in the batter). Gently fold in the chocolate chips.

Pour the batter into the loaf tin and use a spatula to gently spread the cake mixture evenly. Mix the caster sugar and ras el hanout together and sprinkle over the bread, getting it right into the corners.

Bake for 50–60 minutes until a skewer inserted in the centre comes out clean with some small moist crumbs. Allow to cool completely on a wire rack before removing from the tin.

SWEET LONG PEPPER CREAM

Years ago, when planting many dozens of Sichuan peppers, I discovered Christine McFadden's excellent book *Pepper*. It remains a close companion, introducing me to types of pepper I'd never heard of and giving me ideas about what to do with them. I'd heartily recommend searching the secondhand online bookshops for a copy. This is inspired by Christine's recipe and is so good on and in so many things, including the sweet garam masala figs (page 210) and the trifle (page 234).

Long pepper's back-of-the-throat tingle is ideal here. And may I say (not in a shy way) how very good mace and cardamom are together in this. They make a fine pair for topping a rice pudding (page 209) too.

Makes about 320ml (11fl oz)

8 cardamom pods, seeds only

1 generous blade of mace or 2 smaller

3 Indonesian long pepper catkins

4 tbsp light muscovado sugar

4 tbsp caster (superfine) sugar

300ml (10fl oz) double (heavy) cream

Place the spices and sugars into a spice grinder and reduce to a fairly fine dust.

Whisk the double cream until it is just thinking about thickening, then add the spicy sugar. Whisk just enough to thicken a little more.

ROSE, SAFFRON AND CARDAMOM ICE CREAM

Aka bastani. If ever an ice cream tasted warm, this Persian classic is it: rose water, saffron and cardamom are almost autumnal in their comfort. You can make this with the usual dairies, but coconut works so well. The milk is there for convenience: coconut milk tends to come in 400ml (14fl oz) cans, and most of us have some form of milk in the fridge, but by all means make it with 530ml (18fl oz) coconut milk or add a little oat milk if you want to avoid dairy.

Rather than adding the saffron and cardamom to the milk before simmering, adding them just before churning brings a brighter flavour to the ice cream. Some versions of this classic include unsalted pistachios in the mix, but if I have them, I prefer them chopped and scattered over to serve.

Makes 700ml (1½ pints)

5 tsp cornflour (cornstarch)

130ml (4½fl oz) milk

very generous pinch of saffron

12 cardamom pods, seeds only

160g (5½oz) caster (superfine) sugar

400ml (14fl oz) coconut milk

170ml (6fl oz) coconut cream

pinch of salt

1 tsp rose water

Combine the cornflour with a little of the milk to form a smooth paste.

In a spice blender, whizz the saffron and cardamom seeds along with 1 tablespooon of the sugar until it is reduced to a fine-ish powder.

Put both milks, the coconut cream and the rest of the sugar into a large pan and bring to the boil over a medium–high heat, stirring occasionally. Reduce the heat to medium and stir in the cornflour paste. Simmer, stirring constantly, until it coats the back of a spoon. Remove from the heat and allow to cool with a cloth draped over the pan to prevent a skin forming.

Stir in the spicy sugar, salt and rose water. Churn in an ice-cream maker, following the manufacturer's instructions. Alternatively, pour into a plastic tub and freeze for a few hours before spooning into a blender and whizzing briefly, then pouring back into the tub and returning to the freezer.

TAHINI, PRUNE AND STAR ANISE ICE CREAM WITH SWEET DUKKAH

Every year I make blackberry whisky, an excellent two-word recipe. After a few months of infusing, the resulting drink is as delicious as it is impossible to tell of what it is comprised: the flavour of this ice cream is equally opaque as to its constituents, but it is a real smasher. The most common response on tasting is: 'is it spiced fig?'

Makes 700ml (1½ pints)

5 tsp cornflour (cornstarch)

130ml (4½fl oz) milk, or whichever kind you fancy

400ml (14fl oz) coconut milk

160ml (5½fl oz) coconut cream

150g (5oz) caster (superfine) sugar

2 whole star anise

good pinch of salt

40g (1½oz) tahini

100g (3½oz) soft prunes, chopped

sweet dukkah (page 63) and pomegranate molasses (optional), to serve

Combine the cornflour with a little of the milk to form a smooth paste.

Put both milks, the coconut cream and sugar into a large pan and bring to the boil over a medium–high heat, stirring occasionally. Reduce the heat to medium and stir in the cornflour paste. Add the star anise and simmer, stirring constantly, until it threatens to coat the back of a spoon. Remove from the heat and allow to cool with a cloth draped over the pan to prevent a skin forming.

Stir in the salt, tahini and prunes. Churn in an ice-cream maker, following the manufacturer's instructions. Alternatively, pour into a plastic tub and freeze for a few hours before spooning into a blender and whizzing briefly, then pouring back into the tub and returning to the freezer.

Serve with a good crumble of sweet dukkah and perhaps a swish or two of pomegranate molasses.

ETHIOPIAN PASSION BERRY AND TONKA BEAN ICE CREAM

There are those who believe we are each sent to the planet for a single overarching purpose. I used to think mine was to astonish my class by catching £2.37 in small change balanced on my elbow, then I came up with the medlar sticky toffee pudding in my book, *A Year at Otter Farm*; now I realize I've walked among you all these years to bring you this.

I love the passion berries – with their vanilla, clove and passion fruit flavour – coarsely ground, so leave the odd chewy nugget. If you have an intolerance to dairy, I can tell you that this made with oat milk in place of the milk/cream works really well, adding a slightly malty backdrop.

Makes about 900ml (2 pints)

450ml (1 pint) whole milk

300ml (10fl oz) double (heavy) cream

½ tonka bean

24 Ethiopian passion berries, coarsely ground

6 large egg yolks

good pinch of salt

150g (5oz) caster (superfine) sugar

Pour the milk, cream, tonka bean and passion berries into a pan and bring to a simmer. Remove from the heat, put the lid on and leave for an hour or so to infuse.

Return the pan to the heat and bring to a simmer. In a large bowl, whisk the egg yolks, salt and sugar together until thick and pale. Gradually pour in the infused milk, whisking constantly.

Pour the mixture back into the pan and cook over a low heat, stirring continuously, until the custard coats the back of a wooden spoon. Remove and discard the half tonka bean, then pour the custard into a bowl and allow to cool completely.

Churn in an ice-cream maker, following the manufacturer's instructions. Alternatively, pour into a plastic tub and freeze for a few hours before spooning into a blender and whizzing briefly, then pouring back into the tub and returning to the freezer.

PISTACHIO AND GOLDEN RAISIN BAKLAVA
by Honey & Co. (recipe by Sarit Packer)

I first met Sarit and Itamar at a book awards. We were up for the same gong and such was their selfless delight in me winning, I wished they had. Their Middle Eastern food is as happy-making as their company, and I am thrilled they were kind enough to contribute this recipe to celebrate the food of where they call home.

Not long after their London restaurant – Honey & Co. – opened, I made it my business to eat there. Breakfast might be my favourite meal to eat out. As excellent as the main course was, that visit cemented my belief in the tradition of Breakfast Pudding. Their cheesecake – and my breakfast pudding that day – is the stuff of legend, and this baklava is its equal.

Here, cinnamon combines with the bitter almondiness of mahleb – a spice made from crushed cherry stones – to perfect delight.

Makes about 24 pieces

For the sugar syrup

250g (9oz) caster (superfine) sugar

1 tbsp honey

175ml (6fl oz) water

1 tbsp orange blossom water

For the pistachio filling

100g (3½oz) sultanas (golden raisins)

130g (4½oz) pistachios

1 tsp mahleb

1 tsp ground cinnamon

100g (3½oz) butter, melted

1 small pack of filo pastry (200–250g/7–9oz)

Put the sugar, honey and water into a small pan and bring to the boil. Reduce the heat and cook for 4 minutes. Remove from the heat and add the orange blossom water.

Put the sultanas into a bowl and pour over 150ml (5fl oz) of the hot syrup. Set aside for 30 minutes.

Blitz the pistachios to a very rough crumb and set aside in a bowl. Add the spices to the sultanas and then blitz them, with all the liquid in the bowl, to a rough paste. Mix into the pistachios and set aside.

Brush melted butter all over an 18cm (7in) rectangular or round cake tin. Open the packet of filo and cut the sheets in half to create two square stacks of pastry. Brush butter between each layer of one stack and place it in the base of the tin, tucking in the edges to fit. Top with the pistachio filling, followed by the second stack of filo, also brushed with butter between each layer. Chill in the fridge for at least 20 minutes.

Preheat the oven to 200°C/400°F/gas mark 6. Remove the baklava from the fridge and use a small knife to cut triangles all the way to the bottom.

Bake for 30–35 minutes, turning the tin halfway through to ensure it colours evenly. Pour over the rest of the syrup while still warm. Leave to cool before re-cutting into triangles.

CARDAMOM, PEAR AND LONG PEPPER TRIFLE

As I have declared at length in the past, trifle is evidence of a higher power. Should I be cast on to a desert island with only a hungry lion for company and the prospect of one final meal ahead, it might very well end with a trifle, and this might be the trifle.

As is often my wont, I have included some elements separately in this book as they are so good on their own or in other combinations.

Cardamom and long pepper is what drives this along so well, but the thrill of waves of flavour as your spoon works through the layers is really what makes a trifle special.

I save time here by using ready-made custard and stirring half a grated nutmeg through it, but feel free to make your own.

The long pepper cream is perfect here, although I suggest omitting all or half the sugar in the recipe on page 226 to avoid the trifle becoming too sweet.

Serves 6–8 return visits to the fridge armed with The Big Spoon

350g (12oz) madeleines

100ml (3 ½ fl oz) quince ratafia (page 254)

½ whole nutmeg, grated

450ml (1 pint) good-quality shop-bought custard (see intro)

1 batch of cardamom poached pears (page 208)

1 batch of long pepper cream (see intro and page 226)

1 batch of sweet dukkah (page 63)

Tear the madeleines into good-sized pieces and place them in a bowl. Splash with the ratafia and allow to soak for at least 10 minutes.

Stir the grated nutmeg into the custard and set aside.

Halve each of the poached pears and use a small knife to cut out the core. Cover the base of a 20cm (8in) trifle bowl with pears: I prefer them standing on their ends. Pour in around 1cm (½in) of the cardamom infused liquor in which they poached.

Spoon the madeleines over the pears and press the sodden pieces into the top of the pears. Spoon over the custard and smooth over the top. Spoon the cream on top of the custard: make it smooth, swirled or dollops, as your prefer. Scatter the sweet dukkah in generous quantity over the top of the cream.

Eat, ideally alone, with a big spoon and nowhere else to be for some time.

CARAWAY AND FENNEL TOFFEE APPLES

Oh to be eight and staring at a toffee apple large as my fist, wondering how best to attack it, happy as Larry. Making these toffee apples for my daughter over the years and seeing her face light up has been just as good.

Work quickly, otherwise the toffee can set before you have a chance to sprinkle the seeds on.

Makes 8

a few drops of vegetable oil

8 apples

350g (12oz) caster (superfine) sugar

3 tbsp golden syrup

1 tsp white wine vinegar

140ml (4¾ fl oz) water

caraway and fennel seeds

Lightly oil a piece of baking parchment. Wash the apples with warm water if they are waxy and dry thoroughly. Push a lollypop stick or knife into the stalk end of each apple.

Add the sugar, golden syrup, vinegar and water to a large pan and bring gradually to a simmer, stirring just enough to dissolve the sugar and syrup. Increase the heat a little and bring the liquid to the boil, unstirred. Boil until it turns a soft walnut colour. Using a sugar thermometer, heat until the toffee reaches 150°C/300°F – 'hard crack' stage. Turn the heat off immediately.

Dip each apple in the toffee, twisting and tipping the apple to allow the toffee to cover it completely. Dip again if needs be. Sprinkle with seeds and allow the apples to set on the baking parchment. Eat as soon as they have cooled a little.

CUMIN AND CORIANDER FUDGE

I know: you're thinking 'give over Diacono', but bear with me. This is,
I promise, extraordinarily good. There's something of the coffee and walnut
about the cumin and coriander in this, unlikely as that may sound.

There are some key points to making good fudge. The temperatures are
crucial, and the vigorous stirring ensures a beautifully smooth texture, free of
sugar crystals. Lastly, allow the fudge to completely cool at room temperature:
it becomes tacky and won't set properly in the fridge.

This core recipe works beautifully with nuts, chocolate, other spices
(fennel is superb) or just vanilla. You can add the spices early but I prefer
adding them late as this minimizes their infusion so their flavour is more of
a striking punctuation.

If you didn't eat it all in a weekend, I imagine it would keep for a couple
of months in a sealed container.

Makes about 24 pieces

300g (10oz) caster
(superfine) sugar

1 tbsp golden syrup

60g (2¼oz) butter, plus a
little for greasing

220ml (8fl oz) double
(heavy) cream

1 tsp coriander seeds

1 tsp cumin seeds

pinch of Aleppo pepper
or chilli flakes (optional)

sea salt

Lightly butter a baking dish, about 22 x 18cm (9 x 7in).

Warm the sugar, golden syrup, butter and cream in a medium-sized pan – it
should be no more than a third full – over a low heat, stirring frequently to
dissolve the sugar.

Turn the heat up medium–high and bring to the boil. Place a sugar
thermometer in the pan. Keep the mix bubbling, stirring occasionally to
ensure the sugar doesn't catch. The moment the mixture reaches 116°C/240°F,
turn off the heat and allow it to rest for 5–10 minutes until the temperature is
below 110°C/230°F.

While the fudge is cooling, whizz the spices briefly in a spice blender: aim for
confetti rather than dust.

Add a generous pinch of salt to the fudge and beat with a wooden spoon as
quickly as you can; it will cool and thicken, and will gradually come away
from the pan. Stir in the spices.

Spoon the fudge into the baking dish and smooth with a palette knife. After
an hour or so, cut into squares but don't lift the pieces out: leave it for at least
another 3 hours to set properly. Then lift out and sprinkle with a little more
salt and a pinch of Aleppo pepper or chilli flakes, if you like. Store in an
airtight container any you don't eat immediately.

DRINKS

MELON AND PINEAPPLE TEPACHE

If you have never made tepache, a fermented drink from Mexico, it may seem inexplicable that leaving a jar of fruit in water with a little sugar can result in anything delicious, but that's literally all there is to one of my favourite drinks. Most commonly made with pineapple, I love this with melon broadening the flavour and the berries complementing the sweet-sour whole. I use a 3 litre (6 pint) jar, but you can split the ingredients between 1 litre (2 pint) jars if you prefer.

Makes about 2 litres (4 pints)

1 large very ripe pineapple
½ very ripe melon
180g (6oz) raw cane sugar
5 verbena berries
6 Ethiopian passion berries

Rinse the fruit to remove any dust, but not too thoroughly, as you'll risk ridding the fruit of its natural microbes. Top and tail the fruit.

Slice the pineapple vertically through the centre into 8 wedges, then slice off the thinnest 1cm (½in) of each wedge to do away with the toughest part of the core. Deseed the melon and slice into 4 or 6 wedges.

Add the sugar and 5cm (2in) or so of water to a 3 litre (6 pint) jar and shake to encourage the sugar to start dissolving. Place each fruit wedge in the jar with as much Stonehenge-like or Jenga-esque finesse as you fancy, add the spices, then fill with water, leaving 2–3cm (1in) of headspace at the top of the jar.

Fix a square of muslin in place over the top of the jar using an elastic band.

Allow this to ferment at room temperature for 3½ days, checking a few times in the last day and a half to skim off any white fug that may have formed on the surface. It will gradually develop a light fizz as fermentation develops.

Strain and bottle the aromatic juice in sterilized bottles with flip-top lids, chilling it before serving. I often leave a few bottles out of the fridge to ferment a little longer, developing more of a sparkle and becoming less sweet as the sugars are devoured by the fermentation process.

LOOMI TEA

Black limes offer only a hint of their sour, citrus potential, until they meet a liquid. Here, hot water leaches that promise into a dark tea of Persian/Iranian origins, best sweetened with honey (sugar if you prefer). Simple and delicious, in winter or summer.

Makes about 1 litre (2 pints)
4 dried limes
1 litre (1¾ pints) water
honey to taste – try 80g (3oz) initially

Crush the limes a little (I use a knuckle to crush them into my palm) and place them and the water in a pan. Bring to the boil, reduce the heat and simmer for 7 minutes or so.

Use a sieve to catch the pieces as you decant into cups or glasses. Add a spoonful of honey, or more to taste, stirring to dissolve it. Enjoy hot or cold.

GINGER, MACE AND VERBENA BERRY SWITCHEL

Switchels are deliciously refreshing, sweet/sour drinks, initially popular in 1800s USA, especially at harvest time, hence being known as Haymaker's Punch. The classic recipe includes honey, lemon and ginger, but variations are many. Here, the fresh citrus of verbena berries is held nicely by the warmth of the mace with the ginger.

Makes a 1 litre (2 pint) jar
80ml (3fl oz) cider vinegar
70g (2½oz) runny honey
generous thumb of fresh ginger, peeled and finely chopped
1 lantern of mace, broken into pieces
6 verbena berries, crushed

Add the vinegar and honey to a 1 litre (2 pint) sterilized jar and stir vigorously to dissolve the honey. Add the ginger and spices, stirring vigorously to encourage the flavours to release. Fill the jar with water, leaving 3cm (1in) at the top of the jar. Seal.

Leave this overnight to infuse and then refrigerate. Pour through a sieve to serve as it is, with ice.

CELERY SEED SYRUP

There are two syrups in this book – nutmeg syrup (below) and this one – chosen for their contrasting impact, diverse application and outstanding flavour. The first place you should use this sweet, gently bitter, earthy syrup is in the gimlet on page 259; after that it'll be your friend and you'll invite it into the dill honey mustard dressing on page 100 in place of the honey, to add sweetness and depth in gravies, on pancakes and even over ice creams. One part syrup to five of soda water, with plenty of ice and maybe some mint, makes a special hot summer day reviver.

Use this recipe as a template for other seed syrups; anise, fennel, coriander and caraway are all superb.

Makes about 250ml (9fl oz)
250g (9oz) caster (superfine) sugar
200ml (7fl oz) water
2 tbsp celery seeds

Add the sugar and water to a medium pan and bring to a very gentle simmer, stirring to dissolve the sugar. Add the celery seeds and simmer very gently for a few minutes.

Remove from the heat and allow to infuse for an hour, before decanting into a sterilized bottle using a funnel and sieve to catch the celery seeds.

NUTMEG SYRUP

The tiny Caribbean island of Grenada is responsible for a fifth of the world's nutmeg, and there are numerous commercial syrups using the island's most precious spice: as is often the case, homemade knocks shop-bought into a cocked hat. Try it drizzled over pancakes and ice creams, as a cordial lengthened with sparkling water, and in cocktails. The nutmeg brandy Alexander (page 262) is knockout. You can strain out the nutmeg when bottling this, but I like to allow the infusion to continue and intensify: you can always sieve it out later if it's in danger of getting too strong. Store in the fridge for a long lifespan.

Makes 400ml (14fl oz) or so
330g (11oz) caster (superfine) sugar
170g (6oz) soft light brown sugar
350ml (12fl oz) water
2 whole nutmegs, bashed

Add the sugars and water to a medium pan and bring to a simmer, stirring to dissolve the sugar. Add the nutmeg and simmer very gently for a few minutes.

Remove from the heat and allow to cool a little before funnelling into a sterilized bottle, nutmeg and all.

SOL KHADI

I included a version of this spicy drink from India's west coast in my book *Sour*, and spoke about how those I made it for liked it more than I; that it was like putting a track by The Band on a compilation, because others might love it even if I don't. I have been quietly tweaking it in search of greater satisfaction, and here it is; shorn of asafoetida, the garlic halved, mint rather than coriander, the coconut milk to water ratio upped. The result is brighter, creamier and peculiarly additive. I'm still not having 'The Weight' though.

Makes 1 litre (2 pints)

500ml (1 pint) boiling water

14 dried kokums

1 tsp sea salt

2 tsp caster (superfine) sugar

1 tsp mustard seeds

1 tsp cumin seeds

10 curry leaves, fresh or dried

1 garlic clove, chopped

1 tsp dried Kashmiri red chilli powder

generous handful of mint, leaves only

400ml (14fl oz) coconut milk

Pour the boiling water over the kokums and allow to infuse for 45 minutes or so, squishing the pods with a wooden spoon to encourage the flavour out. Break up and squeeze the pods, then drain through a sieve, retaining the liquid.

Blitz the salt, sugar, spices, curry leaves, garlic, chilli powder and mint into a smooth paste using a stick blender, or mortar and pestle. Gradually whisk the kokum liquid into the spice paste until fully incorporated. Stir in the coconut milk and make up to 1 litre (2 pints) with cold water. Taste and season if required. Refrigerate before serving.

GINGER BEER

This is such a fine drink and might be my favourite way with ground ginger. At first glance, it might look a little involved but it is simple and truly delicious. While you can make your own ginger starter, I prefer to source one online from Happy Kombucha and others.

This is a two-stage process, rather like sourdough: first you feed and grow the starter, followed by a second fermentation, in the bottle.

Makes 2 litres (4 pints)

1 batch of ginger starter (see page 266 for suppliers)

7 tsp ground ginger

450g (1lb) caster (superfine) sugar

juice of 1 lemon

Stir the starter together with 200ml (7fl oz) water in a jar. Cover with a layer of muslin held in place with an elastic band and place somewhere warm. Twenty-four hours later – and then every day for the following 6 days – feed the starter with 1 teaspoon each of ground ginger and sugar, well stirred in. Bubbles will appear at the surface as the fermentation proceeds.

At the end of this stage, pour through a fine sieve of muslin into a jug, retaining both the liquid and starter.

In a large jug, stir the rest of the sugar (about 420g/15oz) into 200ml (7fl oz) of boiling water until dissolved. Add the lemon juice, 500ml (1 pint) or so of water to cool it down, the ginger liquid and more water to make it up to 2 litres (4 pints). Stir.

Pour into sterilized flip-top bottles using a funnel. Allow to ferment at room temperature out of direct sunlight for 4 days. This can be a lively ferment, so release any pressure building up at least once a day. Taste it daily too: it's good to see how its flavour changes over time.

The starter may now be large enough split in two, and either given to a friend or retained to brew more. It should stay healthily dormant for a few weeks in the fridge: to activate, remove it from the fridge and stir in a tablespoon of caster sugar and then start the process again.

SPICED RUM

That first half term of big school, I let the slope take me, hands off the brakes for once, down the cutting of the old railway line, feeling like Evel Knievel: one sniff of dark rum and I remember what gave me such unusual confidence that afternoon. These days, the pleasure this brings is perhaps more gentle but no less welcome. The key to this Caribbean classic is to not go too large on any of the spices: too much cinnamon or cloves and it'll taste like Christmas rather than the Cayman Islands; too little allspice and everything won't marry just so. That said, it should be to your taste: try this beauty and embellish as you like. Golden rum is often the base here, but I like this blend of dark and white best.

Makes 600ml (1¼ pints)

400ml (14fl oz) dark rum

200ml (7fl oz) white rum

1 cinnamon stick

4 allspice berries, lightly crushed

1 clove

8 black peppercorns

1 lantern of mace

½ vanilla pod, split lengthways

1 good strip of pared orange zest

5cm (2in) fresh ginger, sliced

Add everything to a jar, close the lid and shake to agitate the flavours. Leave to infuse for 4 days, longer if you prefer.

Funnel into a sterilized bottle, using a fine sieve to catch the spices.

GIN

You may wonder why bother to make your own when perfectly pleasant gin is widely available at a perfectly reasonable price. The answer is – as usual with these things – partly in the pleasure of the palaver, and partly the joy in making delicious seasonal gins to suit where you are, when you are. If I make this in late summer I might twist a handful of fennel seeds or green coriander seeds from the plant; in late spring, I often add a sprig of ginger rosemary or a little of the new growth on the orange thyme; in winter it might be the zest from a blood orange. Because the flavouring comes via infusion rather than distilling, your gin won't be the transparent liquid you are used to; it will glow a pale gold.

Makes 700ml (1½ pints)
5 tsp juniper berries
3 tsp coriander seeds
4 cardamom pods, seeds only
1 tsp anise seed
12 black peppercorns
700ml (1½ pints) vodka
2 fat strips of pared orange zest

Lightly crush the spices in a mortar and pestle to help release their flavours. Place all the ingredients except the zest in a jar, shake well and leave to infuse for 24 hours.

Add the orange zest, shake the jar and allow to infuse for another day. Taste and decant, straining the flavourings out if it is as you like, or leaving in for longer if you prefer.

Pictured opposite.

AQUAVIT

Scandinavia uses such a wonderful palate of herbs and spices that are present but not overdriven with heat. This festive drink shows it off beautifully: cool spices with a warming effect. The length of infusion is yours to choose: taste it after three days and let it go longer if you fancy. Variations are many – dill leaves and orange zest are common – though it is usual for caraway to be prominent.

Makes 700ml (1½ pints)
2 tsp caraway seeds
2 tsp fennel seeds
2 tsp dill seeds
1 tsp anise seed
1 tsp grains of paradise
2 fat strips of pared lemon zest
700ml (1½ pints) vodka

Lightly crush the spices in a mortar and pestle to help release their flavour. Place everything in a jar, shake well, and leave to infuse for 3 days.

Taste and decant, straining the flavourings out if it is as you like, or leaving in for longer if you prefer. Serve colder than a penguin's rucksack.

KRUPNIK

This Polish spiced honey vodka follows a process similar to mulled cider (page 264), and while similarly adaptable, the balance of spices is crucial to avoid tipping its delicate sweetness into cloying. I love this drunk as soon as it has had chance to be chilled after making, though it is differently delicious when mellower after a few months. Enjoy stone cold as a summer shot, lengthened with fizz, or brought almost to simmer in a pan as a winter warmer.

**Makes about 500ml
(1 pint)**
170ml (6fl oz) runny honey
170ml (6fl oz) water
2 cloves
1 lantern of mace
1 cinnamon stick
3 allspice berries, crushed
1 vanilla pod, unsplit
340ml (11 ½ fl oz) vodka
1 unwaxed lemon, halved lengthways and sliced into half-moons

Place everything except the vodka and lemon in a large pan and bring to a simmer over a medium heat, stirring to dissolve the honey. Remove from the heat and allow to cool for 10 minutes.

Stir in the vodka, add the lemon, cover and allow to infuse overnight.

Depending on your enthusiasm for a clear liquid, strain through a fine sieve or double layer of muslin into a funnel over a bottle.

TED'S MOJITO

When I was in my early teens the old man and I were like boiling oil and water thrown together. A friend's dad, Ted, wore life like a Hawaiian shirt; he and my friend seemed like they were old pals more than father and son. Ted always had time for me too: talking, being interested in what I was up to, was I still playing table tennis, and so on. He asked if I might like to come to Butlins with them for Christmas: it was a sanity-saving window of much-needed joy. That Christmas was my introduction to Ted's favourite drink, Bacardi and coke. Whenever I even smell that combination I think of that Christmas and how small acts of kindness can make a big difference. This variation on the classic Cuban mojito is pretty much a posh Bacardi and coke, dressed up for a night out at Havana Butlins. The vanilla/marzipan flavour of the tonka beans links arms with the rum and coke beautifully, with the mint and lime adding bright freshness. Cheers, Ted.

Serves 1

For the tonka bean syrup (enough for 4)

180g (6oz) caster (superfine) sugar

120ml (4fl oz) water

2 tonka bean pods

For the cocktail

ice

45ml (3 tbsp) white rum

35ml (1fl oz) tonka bean syrup (see above)

70ml (2½fl oz) cola

juice of 1 lime

leaves from a good few sprigs of mint

To make the syrup, stir the sugar and water in a small pan over a medium heat to dissolve. Crack the tonka beans with the end of a rolling pin, add them to the syrup and remove from the heat. Allow the beans to infuse for a few hours, ideally overnight.

Add plenty of ice to a tall glass followed by the rest of the cocktail ingredients. Stir and enjoy.

QUINCE RATAFIA

Every autumn, I make quince vodka. Once those glorious fruit have ripened to fill the room with their scent, I grate a few into a jar with an inch or so of sugar, and pour in the vodka. Other than shaking the jar like the happiest of snow globes every few days, there is nothing to do other than sit on my hands until it has matured. Ideally for a year. That 'other than' is doing a lot of work there: it's almost impossible to avoid opening the thing before it's at its best. Last year, thanks to my friend Lucy B, I took a different approach: she gave me a bottle of her ratafia and I was compelled by its magnificence. Ratafia is the broadest of churches with the widest of overhanging roofs: it encompasses a whole world of infused, macerated, spiced and otherwise flavoured alcohols. In this recipe, quince becomes a bridge between the freshness of the last of the year's lemon verbena, the warmth of the star anise and bay, and the liveliness of the ginger.

Makes 700ml (1 ½ pints)

100g (3 ½ oz) caster (superfine) sugar

700ml (1 ½ pints) vodka

3 quince, cut into wedges

generous sprig of lemon verbena

3 whole star anise, broken into pieces

2 bay leaves

fat thumb of fresh ginger, peeled and thinly sliced

Place the sugar and 200ml (7fl oz) of the vodka in a 1.5 litre (3 pint) jar, seal and shake vigorously to dissolve the sugar. Place all the remaining ingredients in the jar, adding the vodka last of all. Seal and leave out of direct sunlight.

Shake the jar to encourage the sugar to stay dissolved and the flavours to be released. I tried this after a fortnight and it was exceptional even that young; a month later even better. Whenever you feel the urge, decant into a bottle, using a funnel, and strain to capture the solids.

Drink stone cold as is, lengthened with tonic or prosecco, and do give it a go with a drop or four or angostura bitters and much ice.

CHIPOTLE MICHELADA

The kecap manis is a departure from a classic michelada, but it works perfectly here. I've made this with lager-style beers from the Philippines to Germany, and while Mexican beer is authentic, it is the quality that is most important. The sriracha as optional: that hot, limey rim is plenty enough wakey wakey in itself, but if you're feeling in need of a kill-or-cure then there can be only one avenue to take.

Serves 2

2 tsp sea salt

1 tsp chipotle chilli flakes

1 juicy lime

1 tbsp kecap manis (page 94)

200ml (7fl oz) tomato juice, chilled

600ml (1¼ pints) Mexican beer

ice

dash of hot sauce, such as sriracha (optional; page 89)

Whizz the salt and chilli flakes in a spice grinder to reduce them to a fine-ish powder. Tip this on to a small plate.

Juice the lime and add it to a jug. Add the kecap manis and stir until well combined. Add the tomato juice, stir and pour in the beer carefully to minimize the froth.

Rub the lime flesh around the top of each glass and dip the rim in the chilli salt. Add a handful of ice to each glass.

Taste the beer and add sriracha – a teaspoon at a time, tasting (if using). Pour the beer into the two glasses and relax, ideally in the sun.

WHITE DALMATION

The traditional Dalmatian cocktail uses black pepper, but I prefer it with white: this is a recipe where the excellence of the pepper shines through particularly well. I use white Sarawak peppercorns. It'll be outstanding with bog-standard supermarket specials, but use great pepper and you'll tell the difference. It is delightfully lively: should you have a slight sniffle or be feeling in any way lethargic, here is your medicine.

Serves 1

For the syrup (enough for 4)

1 tbsp white peppercorns, roughly crushed

160g (5½oz) caster (superfine) sugar

120ml (4fl oz) water

For the cocktail

50ml (2fl oz) white pepper syrup (see above)

50ml (2fl oz) vodka

100ml (3½fl oz) grapefruit juice

ice

First, make the syrup by warming the peppercorns, sugar and water in a small pan until it reaches a simmer. Remove from the heat and allow to cool. Pour through a fine sieve and discard the pepper. Some finer particles may well pass through, but these will only add to the impact.

To make the cocktail, add the syrup, vodka and grapefruit juice to a cocktail shaker filled with ice and shake vigorously. Pour into a martini glass and prepare to be wakey wakey-ed.

Pictured opposite.

CELERY SEED GIMLET

I love gimlets and the opportunity to experiment with different flavours in the syrup. I first made this with anise seed in the syrup as a sort of impersonation of the tarragon gimlet in my book *Herb*, and much though I love it I'm currently more taken with this, at least partly because it is so very much better than it sounds like it might be.

Serves 1

60ml (4 tbsp) gin (page 250)

25ml (1fl oz) celery seed syrup (page 245)

30ml (2 tbsp) freshly squeezed lime juice

ice

Add everything to a cocktail shaker and shake, straining into a suitable glass. If you are without a shaker, use a jar and a sieve.

PONCHE CREMA

Pretty much everywhere has their version of eggnog. The Dutch have advocaat, Trinidad and Tobago has ponche de crème, and my childhood had adverts for Warninks advocaat that promised a lifetime of sophistication. Almost all eggnogs are based on a core of spices, egg yolks and dairy in one form or another; some use brandy, others whisky, many have cream, others only condensed milk. This, from Venezuela, is a delight.

Makes 1 litre (2 pints)
400ml (14fl oz) whole milk
400ml (14fl oz) condensed milk
1 whole nutmeg, grated
1 ½ tsp ground cinnamon
6 egg yolks, lightly beaten
180ml (6fl oz) dark rum
grated zest of 1 lime

Warm the milk in a medium pan over low heat. Stir in the condensed milk and the spices. Bring it to a bare simmer and remove from the heat.

Whisking constantly to avoid the eggs scrambling, spoon a little of the hot milk into the beaten eggs, gradually adding about a quarter of the milk. Pour the mix back into the milk, return to the heat and whisk constantly as it thickens. When it reaches the consistency of thick paint, remove from the heat.

Whisk in the rum and lime zest until fully incorporated. Whizz in a blender on high to eradicate any lumps and agitate the spices a little. Using a funnel and sieve, decant into a sterilized bottle and allow to cool. Refrigerate.

If – as is easy to do – you overcook it and it thickens too much once cold, stir in a little cold milk to loosen it when serving. Serve cold over ice, with a generous pinch of cocoa on the surface if you fancy.

NUTMEG BRANDY ALEXANDER

A couple of years ago, I sat on a coach with two friends, alighting here and there at various Beatles landmarks around Liverpool, the roundabout at the top of Penny Lane where 'a pretty nurse is selling poppies from a tray', among them. Of the many ordinary locations and unremarkable spots made extraordinary by their place in our consciousness, I was struck by Strawberry Field, now a visitor attraction. Back in Lennon's childhood it was a Salvation Army children's home, where the young John hopped the garden wall to play in the grounds. 'They'll string you up if they catch you,' his aunt told him; all those years later he replied that it was 'nothing to get hung about'. The brandy Alexander was Lennon's favourite drink and he always hops into my mind when I have one. It's traditionally made with crème de cacao, but I reckon this is even better. That is, I think it's not too bad.

Serves 2

80ml (3fl oz) brandy

40ml (1½fl oz) nutmeg syrup (page 245)

50ml (2fl oz) double (heavy) cream

ice

½–1 tsp cocoa powder

a heavy scratch of nutmeg

Add the brandy, syrup and cream to a cocktail shaker (or see tip, page 259) with a good handful of ice. Shake until the shaker makes your hand cold. Strain into cocktail glasses, and dust with cocoa and nutmeg. Retire to your favourite chair, where you may well fall asleep happy.

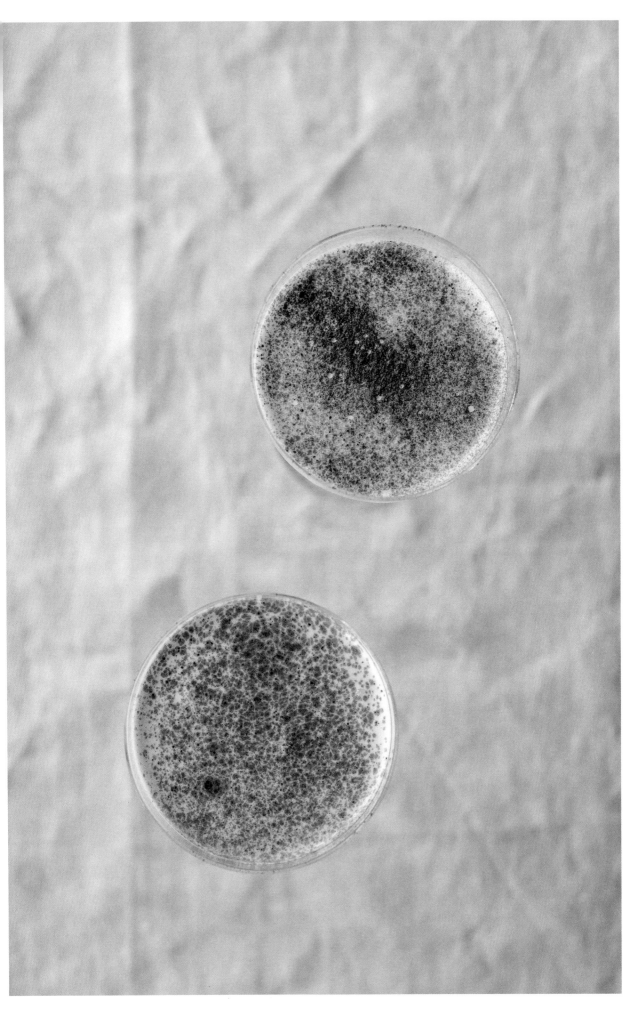

MULLED CIDER

I'd rather drink fermented bin juice that allow a sip of mulled wine pass my lips – too often it tastes like vinegar pot pourri – but mulled cider is very different gravy.

While you can adjust and experiment with the flavours, you cannot dilute on quality: use good cider and fresh spices. Ordinarily, I'd go with three flavours max – e.g. cinnamon, clove and star anise – but here is the exception that proves the rule. As numerous as the spices may be, none are lost to the whole.

Sweeten on serving and a little under what you think, as the spices will give a sweetening impression themselves.

Makes about 1.2 litres (2½ pints)

1.5 litres (3 pints) dry cider

2 cloves

3 whole star anise

6 allspice berries

6 Ethiopian passion berries

6 cinnamon berries

6 verbena berries

6 green cardamom pods

1–2 tbsp honey

Add the cider to a pan, along with all the ingredients apart from the honey. Bring up the heat slowly and simmer for 5 minutes or so. Turn off the heat and allow to infuse for 5 minutes with the lid on. Taste and stir in a little honey if you think it needs it. Serve immediately.

CARDAMOM COFFEE

The only reason I have the nerve to put this in as a recipe – it really is more of an instruction, like 'do your coat up, it's cold out' – is so you don't miss it lost in the main text. It is as delicious as it is straightforward.

Makes about 1 litre (2 pints)

4 cardamom pods, seeds only

1 litre (2 pints) strong coffee

Whatever your coffee is and however you make it, grind the seeds of four green cardamom pods in a spice grinder and stir them into the coffee. If you are using fresh beans, grind the beans and seeds together. Make the coffee as usual, and try it black: I always have milk and yet love it without here – the cardamom implies a sweet creaminess.

TASCALATE

Mexico is rightly famous for its many excellent chocolate drinks. Tascalate – from Chiapas, where the southern tip of Mexico becomes Guatemala – is one of my favourites and differs from many in that it is often served cold over ice. That said, it's pretty special warm from the pan in midwinter: swap the water for milk. Masa harina – finely ground corn – brings creaminess, while achiote's striking colour beings a flash of red and a little of its subtle pepperiness. Achiote seeds are very hard and while soaking softens them, it may be that even with the electric grinder they refuse to submit to forming a smooth paste; if so, stir in another tablespoon of water to thin enough to pass the vivid liquid through a sieve, discarding the seeds.

Serves 1

1 tbsp achiote seeds

45g (1½oz) masa harina

45g (1½oz) soft light brown sugar

5 tsp cocoa powder

1 tsp ground cinnamon

½ tsp vanilla extract

225ml (8fl oz) water

Stir the achiote into a couple of tablespoons of boiling water and allow to soak for half an hour. Blitz in a spice grinder to release its colour and flavour.

Place all the remaining ingredients, along with the blitzed achiote, into a blender with the water and blend until smooth. Serve over ice.

AUTHOR BIO

Mark is lucky enough to spend most of his time eating, growing, writing and talking about food. His *A Year at Otter Farm* and *A Taste of the Unexpected* both won Food Book of the Year, for André Simon and the Guild of Food Writers respectively. His book *Sour* was short-listed for the Fortnum & Mason Cookery Book of the Year Award 2020 and the James Beard Foundation Single Subject Book Award 2020. His book *Herb* was shortlisted for the 2021 André Simon Food and Drink Book Awards. Known for growing everything from Sichuan pepper to pecans to Asian pears, Mark's refreshing approach to growing and eating has done much to inspire a new generation to grow some of what they eat. He was involved with River Cottage, appearing in the TV series, running courses and events at River Cottage HQ, and he has written four River Cottage books.

CONTRIBUTORS AND SUPPLIERS

Alissa Timoshkina – alissatimoshkina.com / @ alissatimoshkina
Annie Gray – anniegray.co.uk / @dranniegray
Honey & Co. – honeyandco.co.uk / @ honeyandco
Irina Georgescu – irinageorgescu.com / @ irina.r.georgescu
José Pizarro – josepizarro.com / @ jose_pizarro
Lara Lee – laralee.com / @laraleefood
Li Ling Wang
Maunika Gowardhan – maunikagowardhan.co.uk / @cookinacurry
MiMi Aye, author of *Mandalay* – meemalee.net / @ meemalee / @themsgpod
Nargisse Benkabbou – mymoroccanfood.com / @ mymoroccanfood
Nicola Miller – nicmillerstales.com / @ millerstale
Sumayya Usmani – sumayyausmani.com / @sumayyausmani
Yemisi Aribisala – @ longthroatmemoirs
Yuki Gomi, a Japanese chef, cookery author and teacher – yukiskitchen.com / @yukiskitchen
Zuza Zak – zuzazak.com / @zuzazakcooks

Ingredients:
souschef.co.uk
spicemountain.co.uk
steenbergs.co.uk
thespicery.com
happykombucha.co.uk

INDEX

ACKNOWLEDGEMENTS

Firstly, let me thank the kind friends – old and new – who gave so much to this book with their thoughts and recipes: each of you has enriched these pages as much as the spices that embellish your food. Thank you. This book wouldn't be as it is without your generous excellence. See the list on page 266.

Rather than declining with familiarity, the more I work with the creative, energetic and dedicated team on these books the more I appreciate their excellence. They bring their personality and creativity to the whole and this book is theirs as well as mine. More specifically, thank you to:

Sarah Lavelle, for bringing together and overseeing the family of food writers at Quadrille and including me in their number; it is more of a pleasure than ever. Harriet Webster, editor and more, for enduring my tangents and not letting anything diminish your humour, energy and brilliance. Claire Rochford, Head of Design: your eye and taste for what works is as keen as ever. Matt Cox, designer and fine friend – what a joy to work with you again, and to revel in your talent. Clare Sayer, once again, for your incisive and sensitive copy editing. Matt Williamson, for working with me on perhaps a fifth of the recipes, and perhaps more so for being a lively sounding board, creative suggester of tweaks and more, and your brilliance on the photoshoots. Becky Smedley, Emma Marijewycz, Laura Willis and Laura Eldridge, and the entire sales team at Quadrille, for your enthusiastic work in helping this book reach a wide audience.

To my agent, Caroline Michel at PFD, I shall bring you a bottle of the gin on page 250 as insufficient thanks for you enthusiastic support and guidance; and to Laurie Robertson, also at PFD: thank you.

You have all made this book such a pleasure to write and photograph.